DIVA WISDOM

Find Your Voice, Rock Your World and Pass It On!

JANE KENYON

DIVA WISDOM

First published in 2015 by

Panoma Press

48 St Vincent Drive, St Albans, Herts, AL1 5SJ, UK

info@panomapress.com

www.panomapress.com

All illustrations including front cover by Emily Harvey

www.eharveyart.com

Book layout by Charlotte Mouncey

Printed on acid-free paper from managed forests.

ISBN 978-1-909623-81-1

DEDICATIONS

To Tony, my number one fan, who inspires me to greatness every day. You are my hero and emotional rock. Thank you for your wisdom and eternal faith.

To two nurturing women, Margaret and Lydia, who put their arms around me and believed in me as a teenager when I so needed some mother love.

To Holly, my unexpected gift, who came to test me and shine a light on my legacy.

To all the women and girls who have allowed me to share their journeys. You rock!

"*Diva Wisdom will make you sit up and listen – for the right reasons! It is thought provoking, informative and a catalyst for change. I believe it has the ability to shape the future landscape for the UK's young women. It is well researched, highlighting many shocking statistics in the world around us for girls. As an entrepreneur if you don't like the numbers then do something about it and drive change – I am joining Jane's Diva mission to step up!*"
Claire Young, entrepreneur and BBC1 Apprentice finalist

"*I deeply admire Jane's dedication to inspiring the next generation of young women. Diva wisdom is a must read for women everywhere.*"
Lynne Franks, Founder of SEED

"*Diva wisdom is an insightful journey of one woman's story and how she went on to use her experiences to influence so many. A truly inspirational read packed with tips from a woman who has clearly, been there and done that!*"
Vanessa Vallely, founder of WeAreTheCity.com, author of Heels of Steel.

And more from Vanessa…
"*A fabulous read from end to end. I was captivated by Jane's "riches" to "rags" to "riches in life" stories. The tips are invaluable, her logic as to the society we live in and the rights and the wrongs are totally agreeable and really shed light on what we can all do to make a difference, not just to ourselves but to those around us. I would recommend this book to any women who is looking for life's lessons from someone who has clearly been there, seen it, done it and has the wounds to prove it. A true role model, a change maker and someone who will no doubt leave a legacy to the many lives she has touched, a highly recommended read.*"

ACKNOWLEDGEMENTS

There are some amazing women in the world doing some amazing things to progress our right to equality, safety and freedom and without them my voice would not have come alive.

I salute the living powerhouses Oprah, Marianne Williamson, Louise L Hay, Germaine Greer, Eve Ensler and Naomi Wolfe for awakening my feminine soul and the gone but never forgotten powerhouses Virginia Wolfe, Edith Wharton, Maya Angelou, Sylvia Pankhurst and Mary Wollstonecraft for kick-starting my education.

Today we have a new wave of female champions and I love them all, particularly Caitlin Moran, Natasha Walters, Kat Banyard, Sheryl Sandberg, Lucy-Anne Holmes, Avivah Wittenberg, Alison Maitland, Holly Baxter, Beyoncé, Rhiannon Lucy Cosslett, Jennifer Lawrence, Emma Watson, Lena Dunham and Malala Yousafzai.

I must highlight and pay tribute to the shocking and courageous work of Laura Bates with her frame-breaking Everyday Sexism project. This book made me cry with frustration, horror and hope all at the same time and opened my eyes wider to the challenges facing our young women.

Another woman who enlightened me on the power of vulnerability and helped me articulate what I already knew to be true deserves credit: the insightful Brene Brown.

Closer to home I am fortunate to be surrounded by some wise and wonderful birds: Emma James, Rachel Ward Lilley, Susan Hamilton and Nina Lockwood. Their support and unwavering faith in me kept a smile on my face even when I wanted to run away!

I am also inspired to live an outstanding life by some pretty awesome men: Dr Wayne W Dyer, Anthony Robbins, Seth Godin,

Jim Rohn and Dr John F Demartini – so big high five to them and their words of wisdom.

However, there are two very special people who light up my life, stand alongside me through joy and strife and have sustained me through the dark days and celebrated with me on the days when it all came together. They are my raving fans and biggest advocates and their love and belief in me means the world. My wise and wonderful husband Tony Davies and my sweet and kind-hearted daughter Holly Kenyon. Thank you!

PREFACE

WHY THIS, WHY NOW?

As I step off the stage at yet another women's conference, confident I have delivered a keynote address, on message, to a group of expectant, entrepreneurial women, the same question greets me again and again as the women step up to shake my hand and express their thanks for my powerful words. 'Jane, you were awesome, do you have a book?' 'Jane, I could have listened to you all day, where can I get hold of your book?' 'Jane, what an amazing journey, love your take on life, is your book out yet?'

Arrrgh! Justifying my answers to these questions has led me here. Here is a beautiful, rustic, remote and totally private farmhouse in the hills of Northern Spain on a mission to write, Jane, write!

I have honed my voice and messages relating to women over the past few years by writing a weekly blog and know for sure I have a lot to say. Thing is now I am also sure it is worthy of being heard.

For the past 10 years I have worked exclusively with women and teenage girls as a coach, motivator, mentor, innovator and change agent. My passion is female empowerment in all guises and my goal is to help women recognise what they need to do to shine. We are all meant to shine. In the words of one of my top female guides:

'Our deepest fear is not that we are inadequate. Our deepest fear is that we are powerful beyond measure. It is our light, not our dark that most frightens us. We ask ourselves who am I to be brilliant, gorgeous, talented, fabulous? Actually, who are you not to be? You are a child of God. You playing small does not serve the world. There's nothing enlightening about shrinking so that other people won't feel insecure around you. We are all meant to

shine, as children do. We were born to manifest the glory of God that is within us. It's not just in some of us, it's in everyone. And as we let our own light shine, we unconsciously give other people permission to do the same. As we're liberated from our own fear, our presence automatically liberates others.'

Return to Love, Marianne Williamson

A wise woman that Marianne. This book is my take on shining. My life, like yours, is littered with critical moments and my lessons have come thick and fast! My intention is for you to be able to dip in and out of the chapters as they take your fancy or as the need arises. The online and offline shelves of book stores are packed with heavy, text-laden books on personal development that overflow with tasks and exercises and I did not want to add to this genre.

So this book is a series of essays, like extended blogs that discuss an idea/view/paradigm; then, where appropriate, may suggest the way forward to change the status quo. But be warned, since I hit the milestone that is 50, I no longer pussyfoot around the small stuff, life is too short. My voice is clear, my opinion is unwavering and even if you do not agree with me (which is fine, I think!) you will be left in no doubt as to what I believe and why.

I refuse to disappear into the background quietly as recent research published via Harriet Harman's Women's Commission suggested I should. The Commission reported that as women hit 50 they disappear from public life, and if considering a career in the media they are on borrowed time as only 5% of all presenters on TV and radio in the over-50 category are female.

I find myself agreeing with Harriet Harman that this is simply unacceptable, and incidentally it also applies to business and all broadcast media.

I AM 50 – TIME TO DISAPPEAR IN A PUFF OF SMOKE THEN?

So, now I have entered the next act of my life at 50, am I supposed to disappear behind a red curtain of shame, mediocrity and silence simply because my boobs are going south and I have a few laughter lines? Think again!

This is another example of blatant ageism and sexism I rally against every week and I am waiting to hear a logical, even reasonable point of view to justify it. All I have heard so far is that audiences do not want to see older women on TV; it costs too much to keep women looking good once they hit 50 and women become too aggressive once they get into their forties – seriously, am I supposed to respond to any of these? Over 100 years of hard fought liberation and it seems clear to me our value is still linked to our appearance and servility. Is it any wonder we occasionally get angry? Personally, I think we need to get more angry, more often.

In my opinion, the older women we do see on our screens are absolutely awesome – they are wise, articulate, measured, dynamic, fun and attractive, and boo hoo to anyone insecure enough to kick up a fuss. Every time I see Joan Bakewell, Germaine Greer, Kirsty Young, Kate Adie, Professor Shirley Williams, Mariella Frostrup, Professor Mary Beard or Kirsty Wark to name a few, my pride doth brim over and I want to applaud them and hug them for their authenticity, emotional intelligence and audaciousness!

Joan Bakewell still rocking

In fact, I watched Joan Bakewell being interviewed by the late David Frost on Sky Arts recently and she was demure, ultra-smart and fun as opposed to Mr Frost who came across as a dithering old man, forgetting his train of thought and having to refer to notes all the way through an hour-long interview. She simply outshone him on every level. There was no contest.

2050 predictions for our girls scary

In the same week this report was presented, more research was published by an independent market research agency on teen girls and their waning aspirations. The Future Foundation interviewed 500 girls across the UK and concluded girls fail to reach their full potential because they are suffering from low self-esteem about how they look. Moreover, one in four girls between the age of 11-17 are weighed down by the pressure to conform to an 'ideal notion' of what is attractive and now spend as much time on their appearance (clothes, hair and outfit) as they do on their homework, on a daily basis. It is not rocket science to conclude this is going to have a disastrous effect on their future careers and our country. This research goes on to predict that by 2050 this national teen identity crisis could cost us well over 300,000 future business women, lawyers and doctors, 60 MPs and who knows how many entrepreneurs.

TIME TO CONNECT THE DOTS

It is about time we started to connect the dots. Old or young, women are being patronised, marginalised, exploited and written off as dolls. If we don't stand up and lead the way, what messages are we sending to our daughters? Our value to society and our personal identity is so much more than the way we look.

As I enter my next act, believe me when I say I will not be disappearing in a puff of smoke anytime soon. Motivating women and girls to define their value way beyond their appearance is my legacy and I shall not stop until we get it!

In the words of the inimitable Mary Wollstonecraft in 1792:

'If women do not resign the arbitrary power of beauty they will prove they have less mind than man.'

I rest my case. Well not yet, I have much more to say on the subject!

IT'S PERSONAL

A lifetime of working with women has taught me how important our personal stories are. I know before you even consider taking on board any of my messages your first question will always be 'So Jane, who are you? What is your story and why should I believe what you believe?' As women we need the back story, don't we? We want to peek in and dip our toes in the water. We want to share each other's journey and then, in fact only then, are we prepared to listen up and possibly take on board some of the lessons. So for the first and only time, the first chapter will be my story to date. It is the only time I intend to do this as, for me, the story may be necessary to gain your trust but the real power is in the lessons.

TOP 10 LESSONS FROM A LIFE WELL LIVED

The first section is a generic set of 10 good habits I know for sure make a massive difference to all our journeys, and even though predominantly this book is targeted at women, this first part is relevant to everyone regardless of gender, status, occupation or age. On first reading they appear common sense but having spent the past 20 years working in the personal development arena I know for sure common sense is very rarely common and only makes sense to the few! These habits take a lifetime to learn and as fast as we master them, another set of life-changing moments appears and we have to learn them all over again!

ALL ABOUT THE LADIES

The next three sections are female centric and build on my experience of working with women and more recently teenage girls via two aspirational brands I founded and currently lead: The Well Heeled Divas and Girls Out Loud. More about them later.

Section Two focuses on what I know for sure about female entrepreneurship – one of my passions. I define myself as an entrepreneur before anything else. I have been creating, building, growing and divesting businesses since my late twenties and my entrepreneurial journey is responsible for many of my life lessons. I have created wealth and sat in the shadow of bankruptcy twice, but I remain passionate about business – its highs and lows, peaks and troughs and dynamism. Being in business for me is like breathing; I have been in charge of my own destiny now for over 20 years and this makes me unemployable, uncompromising and unable to stick at anything where someone else is in control of my future!

I have had the privilege of working with hundreds of awesome female entrepreneurs as a coach, mentor, peer group facilitator and trainer over the past 10 years and they too have taught me so much. Many of their stories, along with my own, have shaped this section and I remain in awe of anyone who steps up and out of the relevant comfort of full-time employment, to risk heart and soul (and sometimes a lot more) to make a difference on their own terms. However, I am also frustrated by the lack of real motion in the female entrepreneur market. Our influence is overshadowed by our fear of risk, failure and debt and our emotional attachment to our business restricts growth and leverage. I have some views and suggestions for getting past this and positioning us where we deserve to be.

LET'S TALK ABOUT THE F-WORD

Section Three is Jane in feminist mode, or as my husband says 'flogging the horse'. I am proud to be a feminist and over the past 20 years I have voiced my concerns and often anger at why we still need to keep our foot on the gas to effect equality. For me, the definition of feminism is focused on equality of opportunity and the right to be free and safe. If you want your daughters to grow up in a world where they automatically have the same rights as men, are paid the same for doing the same job, have a right to decide what happens to their bodies, and are protected by the law if any of these rights are violated, then you are a feminist too.

I seem to end up in conversation about the F-Word with women on a weekly basis, here is an example of how it generally goes:

Chatting with my 28-year-old, high-flying bank relationship manager: 'It is unusual for me to get on with someone like you Jane, you know, a feminist. But you are not like those other feminists, are you?' Well I replied with the obvious and she continued, 'You know, those women that hate men.' My response was my classic: 'Correct Karen, I love men, I just don't want to be one and nor do I expect to be subservient to one.' As I left and reflected on this exchange, at first I giggled then I was hit by a sense of sadness. All our pioneering, such progress, such sacrifices made in order for her to even have the opportunities she now has in a high street bank, and in the 21st century she still thinks we are all bra-burning, tub-thumping men haters (another name I have been called too). This was a humbling moment and is another reason for dedicating a section of this book to our continued development.

My husband and any other men in my circle would laugh at the thought of me being portrayed as a man hater. I am a huge fan of men and could not live without them, but I want to live in a world where men and women are in harmony, where equality is a given, where childcare is a shared responsibility, where choice is paramount and where we are all safe. We women have to get our act together on this one. Now more than ever we need sisterhood, our daughters are growing up in a misogynistic society and our pioneering days are not over.

OUR GIRLS NEED US NOW

And picking up on misogynist society, my final section focuses on what I know for sure about the world our teenage girls are growing up in. In 2009 I set up a social enterprise called Girls Out Loud on a mission to raise the aspirations of teenage girls in the UK beyond a reality TV star, glamour model or teen mum. Since we started facilitating intervention programmes in schools to empower girls, improve confidence, embed emotional resilience and improve body image I wish I could tell you the world is a more nurturing place and there is now no longer a need for our work. But the demand from schools who are running out of ideas to engage girls, control them and/or inspire them grows daily and the statistics on self-harming, teen pregnancies, sexually transmitted diseases (STDs), domestic violence, drug abuse, depression and anxiety, bullying, sexual exploitation, eating disorders and truancy would make your toes curl.

We only have ourselves to blame for this. Social media continues to wreck lives and remains un-moderated; we have mainstreamed porn to the point where young people now get their sexual education from a genre that exploits women; we have normalised teen pregnancy; our media flaunts the perfect body shape and look at every turn; and our public services cannot cope with the resulting mental illness issues and policing/protection needs. Our young girls are in crisis and it is up to us to step up and become role models to show them a better way. This is my hope for this book. My number one. That you will step up and become the role models that they need NOW.

This book represents my musings, my opinions and my views on the challenges facing 21st century women and the next generation. My conclusions are my own, but have been influenced by all the courageous women I have worked with over the years and who have invested in this book by sharing their stories – they know who they are and I salute them. It is not an academic thesis, nor is it a fluffy, feel good self-help rant. It is a status report from the heart, expressed with love and respect for women everywhere. It is a call for action for us to embrace sisterhood again, unite in our common cause, love one another and celebrate our feminine souls. It is a plea from me to you to become a role model for our young girls – encourage them to see their greatness, build their self-esteem and believe in themselves.

This book is all about YOU. So put the kettle on, put your feet up and give yourself a gift – the gift of reflection, refocus and possibly redirection as I invite you to open your heart and embrace your authentic feminine self. She is waiting to be acknowledged and recognised.

My wish for you is that you recognise what you need to do to shine. People that shine are very easy to spot, they stand out a mile, they literally sparkle. Be one of them. Life is too short to watch other people shine.

Love and light

Jane

CONTENTS

PART TWO
Top 10 Lessons From A Life Well Lived

PART THREE
Step Aside Branson The Divapreneurs Are Coming!

PART FOUR
Sssh! The Three Secrets – Super-Woman, Sisterhood & Sexism

PART ONE

MY STORY

THE CRITICAL MOMENTS IN FULL TECHNICOLOUR

Life takes you to unexpected places
Love brings you home

CHAPTER ONE
INTRODUCTION

Critical moments are gifts.
They shine a light on our potential for greatness
and build emotional resilience.

I am fortunate to be given the opportunity to speak my truth at conferences, networks and events all over the UK and beyond and quite often my story will be the catalyst for other women to change theirs. This is a real privilege and a position I accept with love and unity.

In relation to these events I am always asked to submit a quick biography, around 150 words to sum up what I am going to chat about. This is tough but one day I was pretty sure I nailed it and just needed to read it out loud to someone who knows me well. I chose my husband – in hindsight, not the best choice! Here is how the conversation went...

Me: 'Hey Tony, I have been asked to speak at the Professional Women's Forum in the city about my journey, lessons and Girls Out Loud. Can I just read you the bio I am sending them to print in their newsletter to promote the event?'

Tony: 'Sure babe, I am all ears.'

Me: 'OK, here goes. Jane Kenyon, a privileged upbringing to alone and broke at 16; high-flying corporate career to entrepreneurial burnout at 35; wealth to near bankruptcy twice. Her journey is an emotional roller coaster but boy, the lessons are well worth hearing.'

I waited expectantly. Tony took a gentle breath in, put his head to one side and said with love (I think), 'To be honest love, you sound like a bit of a f**k up.'

He then realised from my face he had spoken his thoughts out loud and we both fell about laughing!

Argh! The joys of love and life with your soul mate, eh?

So I present myself to you, warts and all as a f**k up – all I ask is for you to be gentle with me. My critical moments, failures and mistakes have been the making of me, without them there is no story to tell, no lessons to share and no legacy.

CHAPTER TWO
WHO DO YOU THINK YOU ARE?

It's not other people's job to love you. It's yours.

I am the middle child, first girl born to wealthy, working class parents. My mother and father were brought up in seriously poor families in the heart of Salford, Manchester. My mother was a beauty and attracted the attention of my father, the town charmer, nine years her elder, and the guy who was adamant he was going to get out of the slums and make something of his life. He had a few things going for him: a mother who idolised him and worked three jobs to provide him with everything he needed to progress; two sisters who also doted on him and allowed him to take centre stage in all things; a natural charm and gift for getting people to do what he wanted and a smart outlook. My mother, on the other hand, had very little to ease the plight of poverty. Her father was not around and her mother was a tortured soul suffering from bouts of depression that resulted in her never leaving the house. She often turned her angst on her youngest daughter, my mother, the only child left in the house, and was known for her uncontrollable violent outbursts, even taking a knife to my mother's throat several times. My mother lived in fear of these outbursts and spent many nights staying away anywhere she could, her siblings were long gone and she felt quite alone. Today her mother would have been diagnosed as a manic depressive or bipolar and my mother's formative years would have been very different. It must have seemed the only way to escape was to attract a charming prince and ride off into the sunset. My father fitted the bill. He worked hard at school, and even though he left at 14 he applied himself. By the age of 40 he was a millionaire with three successful businesses in the construction industry, a huge detached house in East Manchester, holiday homes, prestige motorcars parked on his gravel drive, a beautiful trophy wife and three kids all at private school. Job done!

However, along with this wealth came a confused identity. My father turned his back on his working class roots, cutting all ties with his family on the death of his father with whom he had a less than smooth relationship. He worked hard to re-invent himself and along with lots of other self-made men of his generation his persona at the golf club and Masonic lodge was a lifetime away from his beginnings. As his middle child I am convinced he and my mother, to some degree, struggled as parents knowing what to do for the best to support their children who had now entered a middle class education system and social domain afforded by wealth. Their understanding of this world was materialistic only and they missed some important nuances in values, opportunities and behaviours that handicapped our development, particularly mine, as my education route was a constant clash of cultures forcing me into permanent survival mode. Clearly my father wanted the best for his kids but was ill-equipped to manage children coming home with very different views of the world and their opportunities than his. He was still working class at heart with strong views on the role of women, children and work ethic. Nowhere was this more apparent than my educational journey. Unlike my elder brother and younger sister I was moved in and out of the private sector from age three to 16. It was as though my father could not decide the best route for me, his favourite child, and my education suffered but my character, in the long run, did not!

From the moment I was born, at home and with my father present, his one and only active birth, I was adored and treated like a little princess. My father doted on me and loved to show me off to all his pals. I was pretty, very sociable with his easy charm and confidence. I have so many wonderful memories of spending quality time with him. Our make-believe role plays where I would be anything from a librarian to a bank manager and he would have to come along to my constructed office in my bedroom and interact with me; dancing with him to The Stylistics or The Four Tops, standing on his shoes while he whizzed me around; accompanying him to a function to be a flower girl, dressed in sticky-out dresses and patent leather shoes and presenting the ladies with a bouquet and a curtsey as he looked on beaming with pride. Sitting on the piano stool watching his hands as he played some jazz or Gershwin hoping one day I could play like him (never happened, despite years of lessons); going with him to his offices in the summer holidays and playing at being his real-life secretary when I was

10/11. I would brew up with authority and strut about as the boss's daughter, very proud of him and his success. I remember the long ride home from boarding school every weekend in my early teens when we would talk non-stop about my week and he would take me to see his latest business projects before we arrived home. The journey back on a Monday morning was quieter but he always took me to Joyce Elaine's, a traditional sweet shop, on the way to fill up my tuck box, without Mum knowing as she would never have allowed such luxuries. As a woman judged solely on her appearance (as I now understand) getting fat was like game over, so I was always made aware of the dangers of sweets and everything was restricted when Mum was around.

From when I was aged four, we lived on a beautiful secluded avenue of 18 new houses my father built. Our house was the grandest and sat at the top of the road like a castle. The avenue was teeming with kids of all ages and it was an idyllic place to

grow up. I, like my father, was top dog here! I was one of the eldest and certainly bursting with natural confidence due to inheriting my father's charm and basking in his love. I remember one summer when I was 10 my dad built me a Wendy house in the garden and I turned it into a school so I could play teacher. It had a built-in blackboard, seating, a library corner, an endless supply of pens and paper and a proper teacher's desk. I was loved by all the parents in the avenue as I entertained, or should I say controlled, all the younger kids throughout the summer. They attended my school where I led classes on reading, writing, sums, bible stories, dance, gymnastics and caring for rabbits. (Most households had a bunny as my dad rescued an adult rabbit one night. She gave birth to 12 babies the following day!)

I was in no doubt that my father adored me and I him. We were not a demonstrative or affectionate family so I never heard the word love uttered nor did either of my parents ever hug me, but I knew I was my father's favourite child. My mother rarely got a look in and I only recall her as the disciplinarian. I knew how to work my dad and I know this made her mad. However, this secret, exclusive, and I now understand particularly unhealthy relationship was not to last. Something happened when I hit puberty: I lost my power over him. My pedestal started to wobble and his need to keep me caged like an exotic bird led to many clashes of will and an eventual meltdown. In the end I paid a high price for his early adoration. But what about my mother? Our relationship was always strained and as a child I was a little confused as to why. She seemed to pick on me constantly, berate me for every little misdemeanour and find new ways of making me feel bad about myself every week. She took great pleasure in my discomfort and tried her best to knock my confidence in all situations. In hindsight with the gift of adulthood I absolutely understand her pain. She was jealous of my relationship with my father, of course she was. I was a precocious little princess and she was pushed out. My father had selected my mother as wife material based mainly on her genes. She was never given any opportunity to invest in herself unless it was aesthetically beneficial, and right up to her death in 2011 she never had any financial independence, self-confidence or gumption. This complex triangle took a turn for the worse when I hit 15. My mother was the orchestrator of my demise but I forgave her very quickly; however, my father's betrayal took a little longer to accept.

During my teens I was in and out of the private/public education sector like a yoyo until I thought I was settled in a small, all-girls independent school in Cheshire. I was happy with some lovely friends, an academic regime I could handle and a degree of popularity that met my need to be liked. It was not to last; for the final time my father decided this school was simply soaking up his money and, in reality, one of his working class values kicked in when he decided academia was wasted on a girl, so for my last eight months of secondary education he enrolled me in our local state-controlled mixed secondary modern school. It was big, scary and full of creatures I had little knowledge about – BOYS!

This school changed my end game from the minute I alighted from my dad's pride and joy, his chocolate brown Rolls Royce. The playground went into overdrive with gossip, who was I? How rich was I? Who was my dad? Was he famous? And so on. That car defined my entry and struggle in that school on a fateful day in 1977 and life would never be the same. I spent the next eight months fighting for my life. I was bullied, victimised and teased by teachers and pupils alike. For the first three weeks there was not a day I arrived home without some evidence of a scuffle – flour and eggs, ripped uniform, lost jewellery, hair pulled out, SNOB graffitied on all my school books and so on. Kids can be so cruel and the need to fit in is so powerful. Being different is only something we treasure as we find our voice later in life.

To be honest, this was my first major critical moment and the gifts were plentiful: emotional resilience, independence and creative problem-solving to name a few, but as in any critical moment I could not see these gifts when I was in it, I simply felt lost, confused, angry and alone.

After one particularly bad day six weeks in when one of the cool, popular girls had decided to make me her pet project and created the day from hell, I decided things had to change. I have no idea where my inner strength came from, nor how I developed the strategy I did but my life got decidedly better once I stepped up and fought back. I had a plan. Step one: make the most of my feminine charm and get the head case of the school on my team. This was a guy who was revered throughout the school and the leader of the pack. I knew he had a soft spot for me so I worked it and became his gal! Now before I continue let's be clear what I mean by this. When I was 15 'going out' meant the odd grope at lunchtime, holding hands after school and stamping your monogram 'Jane loves Mark' on anything and everything possible to confirm your coupling! My strategy for dating this boy was one of protection. I did have some feelings for him but my drive was to stop the bullying and get some respect and it almost worked. Safe to say I was not touched from this point on, my personal belongings remained intact and the bad girls left me alone, but I was still an outsider and I did not like it. At this crossroads, my need for acceptance changed the course of my life. When I ask the audience at my speaker gigs what they thought I did to **really** fit in at this school beyond dating the big guy I get a range of suggestions such as got pregnant, got expelled, ran away from home and beat up my tormentors but none of these are true; the pregnancy one would have been unthinkable in my school days, not so uncommon now though! Let's remember the culture of the school I left to join this mad house. It was a small, all-girls, academically focused establishment where achievement was celebrated and working towards 10-12 grade A 'O levels' was the norm. Now fast track to my new school, to say the culture was different was an understatement. To fit in I did the one thing that would guarantee my acceptance into the 'cool gang' at the same time as creating major grief at home and changing the course of my life. I dumbed down. I set myself on a course to fail everything and I succeeded. Within eight months I had become cool, hip and respected by my peers in one of the toughest schools in the area and failed every single qualification I sat!

Now the critical moments abounded like confetti, my father was resigned to my rebellion and shifting identity. He stepped back from me and approached my future as one of his business projects and decided a job was the best option as a university education was now out of the question as was my dream of becoming a teacher – or maybe I ended up there via a very different route. He hated the changes in me: I lost my posh accent, my friends were no longer the offspring of millionaires, my dress style was different and my social life was no longer centred round the tennis club. My mother was loving my fall from grace and stepped up her emotional abuse just to make sure I got the message. This was her opportunity to regain her position as the queen and she grabbed it. A few weeks after leaving school, a job offer from the Civil Service arrived in the post thanks to connections at the Masonic lodge and I started working in the big and exciting city of Manchester. The job was OK, the people OK and the salary OK but I knew immediately my lack of qualifications would halt any progression and I wanted to do well so I started part-time study that was to last the next 12 years.

At home life was becoming unbearable. My father's disapproval and I suppose disappointment was palpable and my mother seemed to be punishing me for breathing. I was screamed at most days and when she realised I had become immune to her emotional abuse the physical attacks began. Looking back I feel I was the only channel for her anger, frustration and unhappiness; I only had to answer her in the wrong tone and she would flip. I knew this was wrong but had no idea how to put it right and the last thing I wanted to do was tell my father, so it remained our secret until one evening it all got out of hand and we ended up fighting like a pair of alley cats as I decided it was time to fight back. It was horrific and I remember my 10-year-old sister cowering in the corner crying asking us to stop.

My mother's words to me when we pulled apart are etched in my memory even today: 'Well madam, you better pack your bags and leave, 'cos if you think your father is going to believe you on this one when he comes home, you are sorely deluded. You are history.'

Thing is, even though I was not my dad's princess at the time as he was still smarting from my survival tactics at the nightmare school HE enrolled me in, I felt confident that this was my moment. My moment to finally tell him about the unsound relationship that had developed between me and my mum. I felt sure he would know what to do, so after a few hours at a friend's house I made my way back home, at my father's request, to face the music. I was anxious but positive about the future.

The first thing I saw was my huge liner trunk I used at boarding school in the porch and my father sitting on the stairs, a little worse for drink but still very much in control. He was a man in no mood for talking. His mind was made up and I was to be disposed of in as quick and clean a manner as possible. He told me he was not interested in what had taken place in his absence nor did he care for my version of events. 'Jane, I can no longer live in this house with you and your mother. Your mother gave me an ultimatum tonight – you or her – and unfortunately you lost. I have packed up your room and tomorrow I will take you to a guest house where I have paid your keep for six weeks. After this you are on your own. I never want to see you or have contact with you again, nor do your mother or your siblings. Please do not contact us. You are out of my will and my life, in fact if I see you walking down the street I will not acknowledge you. As far as I am concerned I only have one daughter, your sister. Now sleep, we have a lot to do tomorrow.'

I was dumbstruck but surprisingly calm. I told my father with as much courage as I could muster that if this was the basis of my departure I would not return, ever, to which he laughed and said I was incapable of looking after myself anyway and no doubt I would be crawling back pretty soon as I would not be able to keep myself in Vimto! Oh boy, was that a gift! This comment ignited my ambition and independence and it was full steam ahead.

True to his word, the following morning he packed me and my cases into his beloved Rolls Royce and drove in silence to a grubby guest house 10 miles from home. He deposited my cases in the foyer and then drove away without a word and I began the next stage of my journey. Alone. I was 16.

Although this is a tough place to end my childhood years I do have lots of good memories and I know for sure I was loved, so let's move on with a positive finish!

CHILDHOOD MEMORIES TOO GOOD TO GIVE UP!

Never give up your childlike curiosity

I glanced over an article in one of the tabloids recently talking about how as adults we still remember and crave some of the treats of our childhood, things we should have grown out of long ago. Well, who says? I, for one, refuse to give up certain things that remind me of happy, carefree days when I had nothing more to think about or plan than fun!

Here are my top 10 kiddie treats I refuse to give up and when I allow myself to indulge in them, they take me right back to happy times.

1. Tootie Frooties and Curly Wurlys – love 'em and quite often they are my movie treat of choice.

2. Picnics – in the garden, in the park or on the lounge carpet – love the preparation, the choices and the endless opportunity to pick!

3. Staging my own TV show in the kitchen as I bake/cook/create – this is all about role playing and this was a huge part of my childhood. I was a librarian, post office manager, teacher, nurse, actress, dance choreographer, lollipop lady and international tennis player. Often all in one day!

4. Colouring in – I could spend hours doing this and I am not ashamed to admit it is one of my best loved stress busters even now!

5. Collecting things from outside to create something artistic inside – shells at the beach, pebbles from the lakes, leaves and acorns from the garden. I still do this and derive great pleasure from my creations.

6. Doodling with hearts and the name of my current love interest! Obviously the only name that gets in the heart

these days is Tony, my awesome husband, but I could be persuaded to include a certain Russell character or Cruise!

7. Being the first up and out to make footprints in newly fallen snow – never giving this one up. The crunch is so satisfying.

8. Making lollies out of my favourite cordial. As a kid this was always Vimto and I was always shouted at for using too much cordial and not enough water. Ha! No one to shout now so bring it on!

9. Picking wild flowers and presenting them to my mum and seeing the pleasure they gave her displayed on her kitchen windowsill. To this day I love fresh flowers in my kitchen and always try to have a vase of wild blooms from the garden on my windowsill.

10. Party tea – this was such a treat in our house when we could have what we wanted, particularly items that demanded no cooking, on a big plate and eat in front of the TV – this still forms the basis of my Saturday TV dinners!

CHAPTER THREE
MAKING IT TO THE TOP AND STALLING

After confusion comes clarity. Keep the faith.

I know I should have been devastated, lost and unable to function but I felt a sense of purpose, I felt free and all grown up. My father had thrown down the gauntlet and I was up for the challenge. Of course, I had moments of despair, loneliness and fear but I got on with sorting my life, and my anger, although not ideal, was a great motivator.

For the next 10 years I worked, I studied and I climbed; worked, studied and climbed; worked, studied and climbed. I was a workaholic on a mission to reach the top. I was definitely ambitious and competitive but more than that I had something to prove. By age 28 I was in flow. I was the marketing and brand development director for a multi-million pound organisation. I had the team, budget, corner office, car and expense account, along with the responsibility, 14-hour days and expertise in political manoeuvring. Add to this a degree in business studies, three post-graduate diplomas in management and marketing and an MBA and you can see I meant business and had not wasted a moment of the past 10 years reflecting on or getting closure on my abandonment. My therapy was to keep busy but this would prove ineffective as my high-flying career was about to crash land!

At this time I was also in love with my emotional rock Geoff and living in our own home in the country. He was a bright boy and on the fast-track management programme for a major building services firm but he, like me, hated the politics of corporate life and one day simply walked away and set up a garage; cars were his passion. I was not consulted about this but wanted him to be happy so I became the breadwinner while he built a business from scratch. Having supported him for several years I felt it was now my turn to do something for me so I started exploring my options. This proved problematic with such a high-powered job to maintain and I started to feel trapped, unhappy and ill. I had this big job, the big job I had worked like a mad woman to achieve over the previous 10 years but now I had arrived I was stressed, unfulfilled and stuck. You see, I had been on a permanent ladder during the past decade, there was always another job, another qualification, another challenge but once I hit directorship I had nowhere else to go. I was the youngest member of the senior team, most qualified and the upward opportunities ceased. I had to stop and stopping was something I had not done since arriving at Barton Grange guest house 11 years ago.

This is the point when I became ill. I had a funny turn in the cinema one Saturday night where I simply could not move my head. I had to wait for everyone else to leave the auditorium then my man called an ambulance and I was taken into A&E. The diagnosis was vertigo brought on by stress and I was signed off work for six weeks. This was anathema to me, I had not had a day off work in 10 years!

This time out was a life saver. It allowed me to think about the life I had created. I asked myself some tough questions:

Was I happy? – No

Did I know why I was unhappy? – No

Did I want to go back to work and continue with my corporate journey? – No

Did I want to get another job? – No

Was I ready to do some work on me and find out the answers to all of the above – HELL YES!!

I did return to work after 10 weeks as I had a mortgage to pay but my mindset was different and I was tentatively discovering the world of personal development. I had read *You Can Heal Your Life* by Louise Hay on my leave and this opened a world of possibility to me. I had also enrolled on a weekend course called The Journey with an American spiritual teacher called Brandon Bays and I was excited about what I was going to uncover. This weekend was very empowering and was the start of my return to me! What I mean by this is the competitive, task-driven, relentless workaholic was not me at an authentic level, it was who I had become to deal with my grief and loss and it was my way of channelling my anger towards my father.

I recognised my illness as a defining moment and I started to understand the connection between mind and body, cause and effect, and thoughts and things. I did a lot of reading as I also lost my voice for six of the 10 weeks I was off work. How appropriate!

Here are the three key lessons I took on board at this time:

- I became ill when I stopped climbing and allowed my mind and body to actually feel. I compare this to the moment when the common cold/flu attacks. How many of us get ill at Christmas or on our holidays, even as we exit the aeroplane? We all live our lives at 90 miles an hour. It is only when we finally relax we give our body permission to release the negative damaging toxins it has been storing for weeks/months/years. In my case I had not 'stopped' for 10 years, nor had I allowed myself any time to heal from a trauma that happened to me at a key stage in my life. No wonder I became ill!

- I had to learn to forgive my parents for their inadequacies. Holding on tight to my anger, disappointment, self-pity and pain was only hurting me and if I could forgive them I would regain my personal power from a positive standpoint as opposed to a negative one. We all do the best we can with the resources we have at the time. Sounds easy, eh? Believe me it has taken many years and many thousands of pounds in courses/coaching to achieve!

- There is no such thing as an event, there is only the emotion we attach to it. This emotion becomes a belief and often part of our identity and the way we see the world but we can change the emotion at any time with a reframe. The day I did this relating to the moment I was abandoned by my hero, my father, was the day I truly moved on but it was to be another seven years in the future. More about this later.

CHAPTER FOUR
IS IT MY TURN YET?

You don't need eyes to see, you need vision.

Six months on from my return to work I had decided I wanted to be my own boss. I was a highly qualified and motivated marketing professional with a set of enviable transferable skills so I started toe dipping in the world of consultancy and liked it. I discussed my next move with Geoff and we agreed it was his turn to support me, so I handed in my three-month notice and got busy planning my exit. But not so quick, Little Miss Dynamo! Another critical moment was peeking around the corner. Three days into my notice period, my soul mate decides to confess. His business is in financial trouble so he has got a job and is off to Scotland for three weeks on a training course. OK I think, we can do this, he has accepted responsibility and taken action, it's all good. Then my world fell apart. Oh boy, was his business in trouble... in the first week he was away, for the first time in years I opened the morning post. I was not opposed to doing this, it is just that he was always up before me (now I know why) and would leave my personal post on the dining room table before he left for work. The surprises in the post just kept coming and coming: final demands for loans I had no idea we had, most of them in my name; credit card bills for credit cards I did not own but also in my name; tax bills, supplier final demands, county court judgements for garage supplies and the big one – AN EVICTION NOTICE FOR OUR HOME!

I also had regular visits from bailiffs, loan sharks looking to break his kneecaps and friends he had borrowed money from. Once again I was numb with shock but my resilience kicked in and I went into resolution mode. I told no one about this and even during my nightly calls with Geoff my silence was Oscar worthy! I just sorted it. I rang all our creditors and bought some time, I paid back his friends from my savings and I made an appointment with our building society manager and begged him for a second chance to keep our roof over our heads. The extent of Geoff's financial deceit was only truly revealed when I located all my bank statements and unopened post thrown on top of the kitchen units. We, and in particular I, was in serious debt. With a heavy heart I rescinded my notice, negotiated a payback strategy for most of the debts AND saved our house before he returned from Scotland.

I also had weeks to think about how this had happened and the realisation that Geoff must have been living a double life in a downward financial spiral for years made me sad and angry in equal measure. The moment he walked over the front door threshold and saw the neatly stacked paperwork on the dining room table he fell apart. It was like he had forgotten his life here while he was away and the reality hit him like a ton of bricks as he re-entered the house. I said nothing, what could I say? The second man I loved crumbled in front of me and I went through all the same emotions: disappointment, abandonment, anger and resignation.

The only difference this time round was that I forgave him almost immediately as he showed remorse, he was a broken man and after long talks I understood how this had happened. He was so scared of telling me he was in trouble and he genuinely thought he could make it right, he just got in over his head. I forgave him because I loved him. I also recognised some stuff about me in this crisis, stuff I needed to change.

Here is what I took away from this critical moment:

- We teach people how to treat us. I allowed Geoff to manage our financial affairs. I was so busy working and studying I had taken my eye off the ball and this was my wake-up call. I should have known this was happening. I should have known the state of my bank accounts.

- I was too preoccupied with me. My learning, my career, my development and my future.

- I had stepped too far into my male energy and was in danger of emasculating Geoff. He talked of feeling trepidation at the thought of approaching me with these problems and this was a hard pill to swallow.

- I recognised the importance of accepting responsibility. It is fruitless sitting back and blaming everyone else for your life. You create your reality so some of this scenario was my responsibility too.

So life went back to normal, or did it? Within a month I found more debts, despite my pleas to Geoff to be honest and the need for no more surprises. Interestingly, despite everything we had just been through, this was a deal breaker for me and I did what

I have since called 'a Madonna'. I completely re-invented my-self. I left him, I left the area where I was living and I left my job to start afresh in a new city where no one knew me and the slate was clean.

At 29 I started my entrepreneurial journey and I have rocked ever since!

CHAPTER FIVE
BEING THE BOSS

Most people think outside the box.
Entrepreneurs ask 'what box?'

My first entrepreneurial venture followed the predictable pattern of so many. I started a business delivering what I was doing in corporate, i.e. marketing. This was my profession and my comfort zone so I set up a marketing consultancy working in the training sector and later branching out into the business to business market. I ended up providing freelance work for several of my team who also left not long after me and for the first few years I enjoyed the creativity and newness of this business; however, after the initial excitement dissipated I became bored. Not bored with business just bored doing the same things I had been doing in corporate, so I sold this business and set up a business more focused on training and change management working predominantly with owner-led businesses and I started to find my mojo! I have always been a people developer, a natural coach and motivator. The satisfaction of seeing the light go on for other people is what gets me out of bed in the morning.

I have been a serial entrepreneur since the age of 29. I have created, grown, sold and divested nine businesses to this point. Some have made me very wealthy and some have taken me to the cusp of bankruptcy. I have made money and lost it all twice but I remain passionate about business and cannot imagine any other way of making a living. I have run a lifestyle management business, a networking group, a new media agency, a social network and a health business. My lessons have all become clear to me standing in the shadow of failure and some I have had to learn more than once! Rather than repeat myself, my core lessons are discussed in detail in the section on female entrepreneurship.

After working full on for six years my energy bank was depleted and I started to question my purpose. I had invested so much time on my own personal development, I knew the businesses I had created were not feeding my soul. I felt bored, weary and irrelevant. Buddha says 'Your job here is to discover your job. Then dedicate your life to it.' I had not discovered my job and it was keeping me small and stopping me from shining.

At 35 I had accumulated an impressive business track record, I was financially independent, drove a Porsche, lived in a stunning country house set in its own grounds with its own moat, had an active social life, was fit and healthy and had recovered a relationship with my younger sister and was godmother to her young girls. As for love, I was never single but never truly committed. I was having fun but feeling a little disconnected, and unbeknown to me ready for the teacher to arrive...

CHAPTER SIX
MY WISE MAN APPEARS

Whatever the question, love is the answer.

One evening I was in my office, working late and restless. I started to play around with a new internet gadget called ICQ. This was the precursor to social media. It was an online pager that allowed you to connect with people all over the globe. It worked similarly to chat on Facebook but without the bells and whistles, and it revolutionised my dating life! I chatted to men from all over the world and met some great guys from the UK for exciting flings or short-term romance. I even opened the door one day to a guy who had flown from Australia to find me as he thought he was in love with me after chatting to me online for four weeks – seriously?

Anyway in February 1999 I got a message from a guy in London who said he was from North Wales originally but on leave from a position in the United Nations where he was stationed in the Western Sahara and was I free to chat. Sounded interesting and I was happy to be distracted so I said hello. Clearly he was uncomfortable typing and after a few exchanges we switched to a more immediate form of communication – the telephone.

Enter Tony – my wise man, my protector, my biggest fan, my coach, my editor, my alpha male, my love, my life!

But as usual, to be worthy of a place in my story our coupling was no walk in the park! We agreed to meet in Chester one Saturday evening as Tony was making a flying visit to hook up with his son in North Wales before returning to the Western Sahara where he was a UN project worker monitoring the ceasefire between the Moroccans and the Saharawis who had been in a state of war since 1974 (technically still are!). He was living in a tent in the deserts of Southern Algeria, as a key player in a team of workers, supporting 80,000 men, women and children who had fled their country, the Western Sahara, following a Moroccan invasion. These lost and forgotten people had been Tony's world for the previous 18 months and the only reason he was back in the UK was to take a forced break. Oh dear...

On the evening of our planned meeting he called me no fewer than three times in an attempt to deviate from our plans but I was having none of it. I sensed his panic and interpreted this as first date nerves so allowed him some leeway but kept my eye on the prize! His final plea to cancel went something like this:

Tony: 'Hi Jane, I have just arrived in Chester and on checking the train times I am not sure it is worth hooking up as the last train back to London is at 10.30pm and I need to be in London tomorrow to sort my paperwork for my return to work. Maybe this was a bad idea and we should try and meet next time I am on leave.'

Me: 'Tony, I am all dressed up – and nowhere to go now? It is far too late to cancel and I have a big house, you can stay over and make your trip back to London tomorrow, it is not an issue.'

Tony: SILENCE!

Me: 'See ya outside the station in 40 minutes.'

Tony: 'OK. How will I recognise ya?'

Me: 'I drive a red Porsche and I will drive up to the station approach.'

Tony: SILENCE!

Tony: 'OK, I look a little like George Best.'

Me: 'OK, see ya there.'

He was far more handsome than George Best and we connected at a soul level almost immediately. He sensed I was at a crossroads in my professional life and I sensed he was running away from some unfinished business in his personal life.

We never stopped talking from the moment he got in my car and I was particularly impressed at how he cleared a plate of spaghetti bolognaise in the restaurant without spilling a drop on his white shirt, something I fail to do every time! I found his story fascinating – from Merchant Navy to 27 years in the police, forced retirement due to a major assault then moved to Florida for a couple of years to lick his wounds and deal with the loss of his career and marriage, then headhunted by Lord Winchelsea to lead several teams in the United Nations War Crimes Commission working in Bosnia, Kosovo and latterly the Western Sahara. But I still felt there were things unsaid. He was gentle, insightful, attentive and very sexy and nothing like the men I had been dating. He was 11 years older than me for a start and I had a penchant for younger men; he had a beard and I was not keen on whiskers and at no point had I ever dated a police officer – no thanks! He messed with my head for all sorts of reasons, and the morning after, before he caught the train back to London, we went for breakfast in a local café and he told me he had a confession, well two actually. Oh here we go then, here it is, the deal breaker: the Saharawi wife, the pending deportation for unthinkable crimes, the pregnant mistress? I can remember his speech word for word.

'Jane, I know you know I was reluctant to finally meet you in the flesh. That is because I knew in my heart this would happen. I have to tell you two things before I return to London:

1. I am in love with you, hook, line and sinker. I knew from our connection on the phone but meeting you has sealed the deal. You are the most beautiful woman I have ever met, inside and out and way, way out of my league.'

2. I have cancer. I was diagnosed many months ago and have done nothing about it. I was hoping to leave this world in a blaze of glory, as a hero helping people in war-torn countries so I have simply been biding my

time. My cancer is in the latter stages, testicular and now spreading fast so I have been given six months tops.

I am sorry to burden you with this and I absolutely understand if you want to draw a line and never see me or hear from me again but I owe it to you to be honest.'

Now, this was another one of those critical moments where I seem to hold my space and find my inner calm. I did not scream and shout. I did not cry. I was not angry or sad. This was my reply:

'Well Tony, if you are looking for a nursemaid to push you around Disney for the next six months it is not me. But, and it's a BIG but, if you want to live and are prepared to take a different journey, I'm ya girl. I will be with you and hold your hand all the way.'

Clearly he chose option 2 and the next six weeks we embarked on an emotional healing journey together. The timing of our meeting was crucial and no coincidence, as I had just watched a good friend of mine recover from liver cancer through this very process so I knew it was possible, my belief was steadfast. Obviously Tony did not return to work in the Western Sahara, he moved in with me and we have been inseparable ever since. We finally got around to marrying in 2008 and he will forever be my hero and I his guardian angel!

He encourages me in all I do, in fact he has been the main driver in pushing me to share my wisdom with the world. He sees my light way before I do and was instrumental in nurturing my speaking and writing career and he definitely helped to invent the Diva, more about this later...

Believe me when I say like any couple we have had many more critical moments in our relationship caused by ill health, financial pressure, family relations and ex-wives but when your connection is as divine as ours and started so full on, everything else is just chicken soup!

Love trumps the lot every time!

CHAPTER SEVEN
THE DIVA EMERGES

Divas do it with style AND substance!

Following our six-week healing journey Tony and I did some travelling and I put my business head on the shelf. I needed time out as much as he did. Time to reflect and recharge and decide on my next venture, so I divested several business interests and off we went on an adventure.

We spent a lot of time in the States, Tony's second home; for some reason he feels drawn to certain parts of this vast country, in particular the hot arid landscapes of the South and West Coast. With a love of Native Americans I am sure there is a past life over there somewhere! I read tons of self-help books, participated in personal development seminars with Antony Robbins (my guru of choice, every time), Dr Wayne Dwyer, Dr John Demartini and many others and after a few months I had made the decision to train to be a coach. I felt my calling was to support others and help them shine and I had always had a natural affinity for this kind of work so I enrolled on a Neuro Linguistic Programming (NLP) coaching course and threw myself into my next act.

I recognised halfway through the course that I was already a coach; the behaviours, rapport, language and open questioning were already part of my relationship-building approach and I started to understand why I was drawn to this work and how it aligned with my natural skillset. NLP gave me more tools and techniques for my kitbag but the core was already in place.

I also discovered, by chance at first, how empowering my own story was to other women and how this allowed me to connect and inspire at an emotional level. I was ready for the next venture and in 2007, with a partner, I launched The Well Heeled

Divas – an organisation on a mission to inspire a million women to step up to entrepreneurship and wealth contribution, who in turn would inspire one million girls to believe in themselves. At launch we uncovered our Stepping Up weekend workshop, Divapreneur Mindset workshop, Discover Your Diva workshop and Diva Match Mastermind circle. I created all of these programmes and my partner created Divas do Wealth, a one-day programme to complete our initial offer. All the programmes sold well and we had a business!

We were creating some serious brand leverage, hundreds of women had been through our programmes and the Stepping Up emerged as our core product, however relations between myself and my partner were not good. We wanted to take the business in different directions. I was not ready for her online ideas and product development and she was not entirely comfortable with me emerging as the star performer on stage. Although we both wanted to work with women and were passionate about this we started to spend more time debating than delivering and the cracks starting to show.

 Our parting was not pretty. I wish we could have found a better way to do this but we were both stubborn, in need of the control and indignant, and as the business had not made any great income at this point, non-existent cash became the focus of our exit negotiations.

By 2009 I was the sole owner of the business having finally settled on a buyout plan and I continued the journey making some changes to our product portfolio and positioning. This business now became a platform for my personal philosophy on life and I set about nurturing a community of women who subscribed to my notion of what a Well Heeled Diva is – a woman who knows who she is and loves herself. She knows what is important to her and what she wants. She embraces her female energy, lives with balance, love, passion and authenticity and is a role model to other women and young girls. She knows her greatness, embraces sisterhood and shines.

To date thousands of women have stepped up and become Divas through our workshops, peer groups, coaching programmes and community activities and my passion for the Diva brand and women's development has never been stronger.

However, something happened three years into my Diva journey. I realised what I was really doing was creating role models for the next generation. These awesome women who were engaging with our brand and investing in their own personal development all had inspiring stories to tell and I felt compelled to connect them to the next generation. This happened alongside my growing unease at what I was seeing becoming the norm in the classroom. Unless you live on Mars it is hard to avoid the facts surrounding teenage pregnancy, self-harming, sexual exploitation, eating disorders, low aspirations and so on and I experienced a few red flags around this time encouraging me to step up to action. The first was a plea from several Divas for me to coach/mentor/support their teenage daughters which I did with pleasure; the second was noticing more and more mothers bringing their teenage daughters to our Diva Kickstart free taster events, and the third was the speaker requests from schools pouring into the office for me to inspire girls to believe in themselves, focus on their studies rather than their appearance and improve their confidence. I knew I had to do something, I just was not sure what.

CHAPTER EIGHT
THE UNEXPECTED GIFT OF MOTHERHOOD

We are not supposed to know all the answers. We are supposed to let go and have faith in the journey.

In 1991 my brother Richard met Shelley, a local girl, the love of his life and eventually his second wife. You would be forgiven for not realising that when he met Shelley she was a single mother to a precocious, confident three-year-old tomboy called Holly, as he took no interest in her and told Shelley on many occasions he was marrying her and not her kid. A year after meeting they moved into a stunning farmhouse on the estate my father had just bought and renovated, but only lived there for less than a year as a result of the first of many fallouts between Richard and his dad, this one over money. Richard and our father have been in and out of each other's lives for over 40 years but always on my father's terms. This man, my father, has the ability to disassociate emotionally from anyone at any time in an instant. Something I have come to accept as a defence mechanism but nonetheless painful to be on the receiving end of. The three of them moved into a small community of residential properties close to our family home and life moved on. They were married in 1997 and a year before in 1996 Shelley gave birth to a much-wanted boy, Rowan. From the moment he arrived home he was idolised by everyone, including Holly who was then eight, and the family unit now revolved around him exclusively, or so it felt. It was around this time I made a connection with Holly. I sensed she needed someone on her side. I am not sure why as the family was settled and her mother's love was strong, I just felt drawn to her as I recognised intuitively that she was being pushed out. I reached out to a kindred spirit and became the ultimate 'cool aunt'. I spent quality time with her, spoilt her rotten, listened to her chatter and news, and after many a day shopping, going to the cinema and dinner I dropped her off at home in my fancy sports car with the music blaring and us both singing our hearts out! She would jump out of the car with excitement to show her mum all her new outfits and purchases and tell her everything we did, then hug me goodbye until the next time. We were creating memories together. I fell head over heels in love with her and although I was close to my other nieces and nephew Rowan, I knew our relationship was special and somehow her mum knew too and encouraged our bond.

Once she felt comfortable to sleep over she would spend week-ends with me and Tony and her relationship with Tony has always been significant; he was the dad she had been looking for all her life, the protector, the teaser, the educator and the boundary maker. They share a love of films and history and would often (and still do) pull an 'all night filmfest' while I slept!

In May 2000 Shelley was diagnosed with leukaemia and after a courageous fight passed away a year later. Holly was 12 and Rowan was three. It was tragic and Richard did not manage his grief well. He was consumed by his own needs and for years his kids were left to cope alone. Holly became a 'mini mum' to Rowan, whom she adored, and Richard left them to it so he could spend time with his mates on the prowl for his third wife. He seemed incapable of spending time alone and I understand this was his coping strategy but he behaved like a single man with no responsibilities and his impact on his children's grieving process was grim to say the least. Within a year of Shelley's death he was making plans to uproot his family to a new area, a new big house and move in with his new girlfriend and her kids. Holly seemed to cope with this but Rowan started a destructive behaviour pattern rooted in anger that was to last for years as his father broke up with women and found new conquests, always moving them into the family home and upsetting Rowan by showing him no respect or attention. It was heartbreaking to watch. Richard's relationships always took precedence over his kids and he seemed immune to their needs. Only a year after losing their mum they lost the home they shared with her and many of their memories, their close friends and Rowan had to start at a new school. Meanwhile Holly and Richard continued to live in the same house but barely communicated, their only connection was Rowan.

Tony and I spent more and more time with Rowan and Holly, they came to us for many weekends as this suited Richard's social life; however, on one fateful weekend when Rowan was six I became aware of how desperately unhappy he was as he openly shared some serious issues going on between him and his dad that I could not ignore. He was behaving badly as a way of attracting his dad's attention and this was not working as his dad was now in another relationship with a woman who did not like Rowan. I tried to talk to Richard about this when he arrived to pick them up on Sunday night but it did not go well. He accused me of poisoning his kids against him, which was garbage as he had done a pretty good job of that without my help! He told me in no uncertain terms to back off and I saw very little of Rowan from this point on. Over the years I have watched Rowan self-combust from a distance. He is now 17, living independently and in trouble. His dad kicked him out after an argument when he was 16 – see any patterns here?

At 16 Holly started college and was barely surviving living with Richard and Rowan. The atmosphere at home was toxic and her relationship with Richard was all but finished. She only stayed to support her beloved Rowan and spent as much time as she could with Tony and me. True to type Richard became defensive about our growing closeness and kicked her out. Like father, like son eh? How does the saying go: you either repeat or rebel?

At 18 Holly became the first girl on her side of the family to go to university and off she went like an excited puppy to start her independent journey. This was the first time in her life when her only responsibility was herself and she faltered at the first hurdle. She did not cope living away from home and her first taste of freedom focused on alcohol, drugs and truancy. Needless to say, she secretly failed her first year but was given a second chance which she also failed as she simply did not do the work. We had no idea this was going on; on her regular visits home and summer vacation she was full of excitement and stories about 'uni life' and seemed deliriously happy, but in June 2010 she went missing and all communication stopped. This was torture for us as we had no idea where she was or why she was silent. All her university friends had returned home for the summer so no one knew her whereabouts. We even sent the local police to her digs and they reported back to confirm she was there, but still no contact.

Finally, 13 weeks later in September 2010 I received a very distraught phone call from her gran (Shelley's mum) to say she had showed up at her house, very depressed and non-communicative and she did not know what to do with her. She thought she was having a mental breakdown and asked me to come and get her. I did and at 18 Holly started the long, painful journey of delayed grief, loss and closure. She was angry at her mother for marrying Richard and even more angry at her for leaving her with him. She was struggling to find her identity. She was now our daughter and yet felt guilty about her love for us and still felt responsible for leaving Rowan. We have worked through a lot of this together but I know from experience I cannot fix her, nor can I continually rescue her. She needs to own her journey and now aged 25 she is finally starting to see the light. I remain positive that Rowan will also find his path sometime soon.

I feel privileged to have been given the chance to be a mother to Holly. In the final week of her mother's life in a sterile hospital room in Christies, Manchester, Shelley pleaded with me to look out for Holly and it has never been a chore. Her mum knew Richard well. She knew intuitively he would not be single long and she also knew he had never accepted Holly. I was her security, her ace card. She knew I loved Holly and would make her my number one. She was right. God bless you Shelley.

Holly has taught me so much about myself and been instrumental in me recognising my affinity and passion for supporting troubled teens. I inherited a broken teenager and she helped me open the door to my legacy. Amen to that!

CHAPTER NINE
ENTER THE TEEN CHAMPION AND SOCIAL ENTREPRENEUR

Business today is about making a difference.
Everything else is wallpaper.

In 2008 I was invited to speak at a national conference for young people called STEP UP in Blackpool. Blackpool has always been a town with youth employment challenges, low aspirations and high teen pregnancies and a charity supported by the council was hosting a motivational event for over 2,000 teens to help build confidence and resilience. The idea was to invite around 12 speakers with a motivational story to tell, people who had some adversity in their youth, but had overcome this and were now successful. These speakers would share their stories from the heart with a view to inspiring the teens that anything is possible. The message: if it's possible for me, it's possible for you. It's simply a question of how. All our stories are different. I was honoured to be invited to participate and even more in awe when I realised I was one of only two female speakers on stage.

My session was to be the catalyst for the next stage in my journey. My impact on the girls in the audience was so powerful I was invited into more schools to present but I did not want to do this anymore. I knew an hour's motivational presentation was only scratching the surface at some of the deeply embedded issues and limiting beliefs at play here and I needed more. Fortunately I was introduced to two amazing women, Nicola Hall and Alison Sadler, who were leading a social enterprise in Blackpool called HERO and who totally shared my passion for raising the aspirations of teenage girls. They provided the school, the girls and the funding to allow me to pilot, develop and deliver a five-month intervention programme with a group of disengaged, troubled and vulnerable girls. Girls Out Loud was born.

If I am honest I had no idea if my experience, knowledge and skills from a decade of working with women would translate to teenage girls. I spent a month planning a loose structure and exercises but I did not know if the intervention would work or if I was capable of delivering it. As usual, Tony had full faith in me and kept saying 'Jane, just be you, they will respond to you, they will see your passion and know you care, just be you.' And as usual, he was right, although many times on my journey home from spending four hours with them all I would be wracked with doubt and the tears flowed as I struggled to comprehend the complexities of their life and wondered if I was really helping them.

This intervention programme was made up of a weekly four-hour session with the full group of girls ending with us eating tea together, then each girl spent quality one-to-one time with me each month in a coaching relationship. By the end of month 2 when I started to see some real shifts in the girls' outlook and self-esteem I realised this was my real legacy. I was reminded of one of Oprah's mantras all the time as I worked with these girls: 'All anyone really wants is to be seen, to be heard and to know that what they say matters.' This is called validation or recognition and we all desire it and will often look for it in the wrong places. I refer to this as finding your voice and it is the cornerstone of all my work with girls and women alike.

These girls from the first programme inspired me to create the social enterprise Girls Out Loud to raise the aspirations of teenage girls in the UK. The organisation launched in 2010 with myself and Claire Young as co-founders. Claire is the straight-talking, no-nonsense sales woman who infuriated then won over 11 million viewers to reach the final in series 4 of BBC1's The Apprentice (2008). Since then she has worked non-stop setting up numerous businesses.

Girls Out Loud has grown exponentially year on year since then. However, in 2011 Claire stepped back due to work commitments and the arrival of her first child. I have continued to build the team and create momentum and in 2011 we launched a Big Sister mentoring programme to complement our other intervention programmes we deliver in schools across the country all focused on creating a more empowering mindset in our girls. We aim to improve confidence, self-esteem and body confidence and embed emotional resilience and aspiration. Finally I had the perfect platform to introduce my awesome Diva posse to girls!

Girls Out Loud is my legacy project. I spend most of my working week creating attraction to this brand, talking to corporates to foster partnerships and participation; motivating women to step up and volunteer to be a role model to a young girl; recruiting and training coaches to deliver the Stardom programme I originally piloted in Blackpool; leading a team of thousands of female volunteers supporting our cause; appointing some awesome women to act as Ambassadors for our brand; talking to schools about how we can support their work; talking to the press about our much-needed work. Every day brings more challenges as the demand for our programmes increases and the funding disappears but we will not be deterred. We know we make a difference, we have the girls' stories and successes to prove it and we will continue on our mission to be the leading provider of motivational programmes utilising the stories and commitment of real role models, for teenage girls in the UK.

CHAPTER TEN
THE NEXT ACT

Life does not begin at 21, 30, 40, 50 or beyond.
It begins when you say so!

I absolutely believe that my life has purpose and everything that has ever happened to me, good or bad, has resonance and an intention. I could not do what I do, I would not be who I am or attract what I attract without my life journey and lessons. I have peace and closure on a complex and traumatic family breakdown; I attracted the man I have been waiting for all my life when I was ready; I am incredibly lucky (if you believe in luck) to wake up every day with bliss to be able to do what I love and I am well on the way to creating a legacy that will survive long after I am gone.

My number one watch word and value is AUTHENTICITY and this is how I try to live my life. I no longer spend hours worrying about what people may think of me, life is too short and I believe I have earned the right to express my opinion, show my vulnerability, say no or walk away.

As I hit 50 and the next stage of my life is in view, I know for sure I want to spend more quality time with my husband, travel more and step back from hands-on delivery, increase my influence within my niche and slow down the manic pace of my life from 90 miles an hour to around 60!

THINGS I KNOW FOR SURE AT 50

1.   That love is far more important than money ANY day of the week. Yes I hear you say, it is no fun to be broke but so long as you have people who love you to share being broke, life will and always does get better. True wealth is what's left when the money runs out!

2. That my intuition is worth more than every qualification I have studied long and hard for and believe me I have many. Most of the business mistakes I have made have all happened when I have ignored or overridden my intuition.

3. That imitation is the highest form of flattery and no longer a threat to me. I know for sure my style, substance and passion is unique and you may copy what I say and what I do but you will never do it the way I do it, nor leave the same footprint. I finally understand I am an artist! Thank you Seth Godin for your amazing book *The Icarus Deception* that shone the light on my individuality.

4. That common sense is not always common and it generally only makes sense to you!

5. That authenticity is the end game, the Holy Grail and the purpose of ALL personal development. We are all searching for our voice, our true self in everything we do, feel and say. I found mine many years ago and refuse to compromise or marginalise it for anyone or anything. This has demanded courage at many times in my life and has meant I have had to say goodbye to some people, but if I am not true to me what is the point of my life?

6. That feminism and sisterhood has never been more important. All over the world, every day women and girls are raped, abused, beaten and exploited. Closer to home domestic violence is commonplace, the media is a playground for porn and misogyny and women are almost invisible at the top in all areas of corporate and public life. Our pioneering is not over and now is not the time to take our foot off the gas. The next generation deserve our continued vigilance and campaigning.

7. That life begins at the end of your comfort zone. If you are not risking you are not living. This takes gumption but I know the alternative of settling for mediocrity or simply cruising makes me play small and makes me miserable!

8. That the family you are born into is not necessarily the place you will find unconditional love, respect, joy and validation. I now have very little to do with my blood family, it has been a long and painful journey but the family I have created makes up for all the disappointment and stress a million times over. I consider myself loved and blessed.

9. That emotional resilience is a fundamental skill needed to live your best life but can only be honed by failing and making mistakes. Failure is the gift that allows us to learn lessons and shift our mindset. I am grateful for all my failures, even the frame-breaking ones, as without them my lessons would have remained hidden and I would never have found my true calling or my strength.

10. That passion is contagious and life affirming and under no circumstance should you ever give up searching and exploring the reason why you are here. I found my purpose in my late thirties when I found my niche helping women step up and shine. This work led me to work with teen girls and the rest, as they say, is history!

CHAPTER ELEVEN
FAQ – LEAVE 'EM WANTING MORE, EH?

Strength comes from knowing who you are,
courage is a habit.

So do you have any questions so far? Have I missed any key points along the way? Generally when I share my story with an audience and we arrive at the questions section I can predict the first few out of the bag! So here are the top hand-raisers. If I have missed your burning question just email me, all my details are at the back of the book.

1. Jane, do you have a relationship with your family now?

There is a short answer and a long answer to this one but seeing as I have the luxury of time and space I reckon you deserve the long one! The short answer is NO. The long one is self-induced purgatory lasting well over 30 years. I have held the olive branch out to both my parents so many times I have lost track, but without fail every time they have simply snatched it out of my hand and beaten me up with it! I have had moments where we are on speaking terms, no emotional connection but able to exchange pleasantries if we were in the same room at a family function; others where I managed to have a reasonable conversation, and years of complete estrangement.

I have been their marriage counsellor when my father was on the brink of having an affair and my mother rang me at work and asked me to come home and talk to him. I was the mediator when my sister wanted to move in with her boyfriend and my father refused to allow it. I am the only one of their children not scared to voice an opinion or question my father as I am not afraid of him nor am I waiting for his inheritance or approval. Some days I think he respects this and others he deplores it.

My first contact with my father post-16 was an interesting ex-change and one that revealed the hill I was going to have to climb over and over again if I expected to recover a relation-ship. I was 19, feeling very low after surgery on my throat and decided to take my counsellor's advice and write a letter to my father telling him how I felt. She suggested this would be a good way to release the noise in my head and help me let go of my anger. The letter was several pages long and not particularly pleasant in content or language. It was definitely cathartic to write but I did more than write it, in a spontaneous moment I posted it. This was not part of the plan but hey ho! A few days later I returned from work to the shared house I was renting and one of my housemates asked me if I had a sugar daddy. 'Think not,' I replied – 'why?' She then went on to describe my dad and told me this very handsome, tanned man had been sit-ting in a Range Rover round the corner for the past two hours. I went out to the car and invited him in. This was it, the rec-onciliation, the chance to talk, the opportunity to win my dad back! He was not on the same page! He walked in, threw the letter at me and said my life choices were upsetting my moth-er and clearly I was not capable of looking after myself as the letter showed. He suggested this was a cry for help and that it was time to come home. I was in shock. How had he interpret-ed that letter as a cry for help? The life choices he referred to were my relationship with a divorced man and living in a less than middle class area. I remained calm and explained I did not think it was a wise move to come home, especially since I had now experienced independence. He said, 'You are coming home and as long as you live under my roof, my rules apply, get your stuff, I will be in the car.' I took a deep breath and said 'no thanks.' I did not see him again for four years, the time I reconnected with my sister after a chance meeting in town. His recollection of this conversation was so outlandish and untrue all I could do was laugh out loud when he recounted it to me. He remembered me defining a list of demands for my return home including a deposit of £20k into my bank account and a brand new Porsche! This was so preposterous but clearly a version created to ease his guilt and smooth his conscience. Beliefs are anything but objective, eh? We create our own interpretations of what we see and hear all the time, maybe my version of events is filtered too, but anyone who knows me will tell you I am fiercely proud and even more stubborn and no way would I ever ask my father for money. On several occasions when I have tried to get closure, or understand my father's thinking, his version of events is so unjust and untrue I end up in a worse place emotionally than I was when I asked! I have learned to let go and Tony has helped me move on as his objective take on the situation has been all the validation I needed.

The relationship with my mother was so broken and misunderstood we never really got it together and this is one of my regrets. As I matured and became more self-aware I absolutely understood the pernicious foundation of her relationship with my father, and whilst I was in no doubt of their love and dependency for one another, I know she must have found his controlling attitude claustrophobic. We had moments of closeness when she confided in me and I know she was close to leaving him once but was too scared as she had never been alone, had no money of her own and my father threatened her with poverty, pressing all the right buttons to keep her in place. I forgave her for all her anger towards me with ease. Her upbringing told me she knew no better and she always believed she had provided a great life for her children. I know she must have looked at my life with envy – my independence, my career, my ability to speak up and own my voice, my gumption and my spirit. She died in 2011, in her home in Spain, after suffering for several decades with ill health and this was the point I severed all links with my family as I was banned from attending her funeral by my father and both my brother and sister colluded with him to make sure I stayed away. My relationship with my brother has always been tenuous, so his betrayal was of no consequence, but I was close to my sister and her girls and I found her act unforgivable, so after 30 years of banging my head against a brick wall, I finally closed the door. No more Jane, no more.

The foundation of my family unit is toxic. We are emotionally dysfunctional with parents who had such complex, hard and in my mother's case loveless upbringings that to show emotion or to understand and teach love is problematic. You don't know what you don't know and I truly believe my mum and dad did the best they could do with the resources they had. I was blessed to have an excellent education until the final year and even that taught me survival! I know what it feels like to be adored, so attracting this into my life has been easy, and even though I had a tough time the positives far outweigh the negatives and I have gratitude for all the love and lessons.

The most important family to me is the one I have created: my husband, my niece, my close friends and my extended family of Divas and Divas-in-Waiting (teen girls). I am surrounded by love, passion and adventure and all is well.

2. Jane, do you think entrepreneurs are born or created?

As you will read in the section on female empowerment I believe entrepreneurship is 100% mindset so I believe it is learnt behaviour and if the passion and purpose are in place anyone can build a business. However, we do not all build businesses in the same way. I am a creator, a high energy visionary with a big picture mentality, a need for people interaction and no interest in detail. I have met successful entrepreneurs who display the complete opposite set of traits, so be careful not to judge everyone on the characteristics of Branson or Gates. More about this when we talk about Wealth Dynamics.

However, I also believe some people are more predisposed to being their own boss than others and this can be related to their upbringing, education or role models. My role model growing up was my father. I idolised him and wanted to be like him when I grew up – the boss. I saw and admired his work hard, play hard mentality and I only ever knew him as a business man. This was normal to me so it makes sense that I would follow his lead. I am also a self-confessed control freak like him, so I find it hard being told what to do or fit into a structure that limits my autonomy and/or creativity. Maybe if he was a doctor I would be one too?

3. Tony's healing process sounds amazing, is he still well?

It was amazing and we live in eternal gratitude but it was no walk in the park. He spent six weeks unlocking emotional blocks and reframing baggage from over 40 years! This takes some courage and tenacity to see through and I am in awe of his capacity to manage his fear. After six weeks we arrived at a local hospital in Manchester for his check-up and were kept waiting hours as the medical team went over and over his scans and tests looking for a tumour that was no longer there! At this point I was elated but to my surprise Tony entered a black hole of depression that took more work and longer to climb out of than the original healing journey. He felt cheated, he was supposed to die. He now had a brand new list of things he needed to deal with, he had not dealt with any of his financial affairs, he lost his career and marriage due to this illness and now people were telling him it had vanished.

We worked through this together too and Tony has been cancer free ever since. He has suffered from other health scares, in fact I nearly lost him to a severe stomach hernia in 2010 but it is not his time yet and our love affair continues.

4. Who is your role model, Jane?

Obviously as I mentioned before, when I was growing up my father, for sure. These days I am inspired by anyone who has overcome adversity or is making a difference. I am a huge fan of Oprah and Anthony Robbins and in business Jamie Oliver, Jo Malone, Richard Branson and Seth Godin.

5. Where does your self-belief come from, Jane, it is awesome!

Where does anyone's self-belief come from I wonder? I have been tested from a young age. My early years were rich in positive validation from my father and I was in no doubt that I was bright and charming and a social success, so this must matter. My troubled teen years were the foundation for my confidence, emotional resilience and strength of character and I have invested so much time, money and energy in my own personal development some of it has to rub off some time!

I have always been happy with who I am and my sense of self has always been strong. Even in the shadow of failure and in critical moments I have always felt sure that I will prevail.

6. What is your definition of success, Jane, and are you motivated by money?

No I am definitely not motivated simply by money. I was brought up in a wealthy family with no great benefit emotionally, mentally or otherwise. I was well educated yet still alone and broke at 16. Furthermore, throughout my entrepreneurial journey I have ridden the wealth to near bankruptcy roller coaster at least twice and survived!

Clearly, money does not define success for me! However, don't get me wrong, I am not a fan of poverty either. The world has enough poor people, we need capable, motivated people to step up and create wealth more than ever today but, and it's a BIG BUT, the majority of wealth on display in the Rich Lists of the western world is not making a difference or contributing to society in any way, shape or form. It is paying for £25k an hour tax lawyers; £21m weddings (yes I said £21 million); £24k private car registration plates, £2m walk-in wardrobes and so on. I have no issue with people who make millions and people who spend millions, I just wish they understood the power of their wealth and the difference their philanthropy could make to the world, as well as enjoying the finer things in life.

Now before you start quoting the stories of Branson, Gates, Oprah, JK Rowling and Warren Buffet, I am well aware of and inspired by these enlightened entrepreneurs who, like me, subscribe to wealth contribution and social enterprise, but believe me they are in the minority. For every Branson there are thousands of seriously wealthy individuals and families who do nothing with their cash other than over indulge, over consume and overcharge our environment!

Now to my definition of success. For me **true wealth is what's left when the money has gone!**

I consider these things to include a positive and empowering mindset, emotional resilience, health, friends, family and peers, passion, wisdom, self-belief and connections. No matter what happens in life, if you have invested in these things you will be able to recover from anything and reinvent yourself at will. So for me failure is not the end, it is simply a lesson, a stop along the way, a chance to reflect and recharge. Many entrepreneurs feel the same way and are proud of their failures, it makes them stronger, more resilient and hones their passion.

So, my definition of success? For me, it is about personal growth, influence, connection, passion, authenticity and love. Successful people come from all walks of life but tend to stand out – their energy and passion is palpable, they infect their environment, their love of self and life is contagious. These are the people I choose to hang around with and if they are also financially wealthy then so be it. The two are not mutually exclusive and you can be sure if they are in my peer group they will be using their wealth in a positive way to change the world.

PART TWO
TOP 10 LESSONS FROM A LIFE WELL LIVED

Be bold, be brave, be the authentic you, because you are enough

INTRODUCTION

Dump good and step up to outstanding today.

I fully subscribe to Anthony Robbins' view on life, he is an exceptional human being, an awesome motivator, insightful, emotional and smart and simply the best speaker I have ever seen in action. His Life Mastery University has been instrumental in my journey and this is definitely one of his mantras I live by: Most people settle for good but these days good equates to average and who wants to be average? The difference between good and outstanding is tiny in terms of input but massive in terms of output. People who subscribe to outstanding make up around 5% of the population and recognise that they need to stand out and go the extra mile in all things, but in reality this is not so difficult as most people are simply cruising along and staying within their comfort zone. People living an outstanding life take more risks, they continue learning about themselves and their capabilities, they work on improving their mindset and self-esteem and they surround themselves with other outstanding people to ensure their energy is not infected by negative moaners! In short, they invest in themselves on a continuous basis. This is the inputs sorted but what about the output? Outstanding people live large! They attract more, they earn more, they love more and they give more. In essence the difference between good and outstanding is a senior management position versus a seat round the top table; someone who delivers the law versus someone who makes it; someone who hosts their own TV show versus someone who owns the network.

We can all step up to outstanding at any time and to be honest when you consider the advantages why would anyone settle for good? The following section is my take on what you need to master to step up to outstanding and join the 5%. They represent my core lessons and the blueprint for how I live my life. Take from them what you need and remember, life begins at the end of your comfort zone not in it!

LESSON ONE

*I know for sure in our critical moments
our identity is shaped*

Life is full of moments where we are forced to stop and change direction in some way. It could be something as simple as the day your last child leaves for university and the house is quiet, or the moment you realise your relationship is over, or your money runs out before the end of the month. The bigger moments like the death of a loved one or a business failure demand more courage to recover from but it is in these moments that we come face to face with who we are and what we are capable of. We have to make choices. We can decide to step up or step back, stand tall or shrink, play full out or opt out. We find out who our friends are, what and who is important to us, where our loyalties lie and we recognise whether our current life choices are working.

The more self-aware you are the quicker you recover from these moments because you can identify the way out faster. For example, if you are already living your life aligned with your values, when the critical moment arrives this is one less thing to soul search about. The same if you are on purpose, living with passion, the choices and decisions are more obvious. If you already have an inspiring, supportive peer group on board you have an outlet for advice and a pipeline to source more wisdom. Does this make sense?

Every critical moment you face and work through builds emotional resilience and teaches you something about yourself. This then becomes part of your identity but here's the thing. If you are not living your best life and taking some personal risks then your critical moments are likely to be frame breaking and irregular – i.e. they don't come often but when they do it is total meltdown. Put another way, if all you ever do is go with the flow, eventually you will end up at a waterfall by which time it's too late to do the work. If you are living on the edge of your comfort zone, critical moments come thick and fast because you are really putting yourself out there, investing in your personal development and creating an outstanding life.

In February 2012 I had a nasty fall and seriously damaged my knee. After surgery I was in a wheelchair for a week, then on two crutches for six weeks, one crutch for four weeks and then a stick for another four weeks. This was a long recovery process and definitely a critical moment! However, as an entrepreneur I had to carry on working and I was in the middle of two major projects. The first was an event I was leading for a regional women's charity I am a founder of called The Birdhouse Fund. The event was called 'Manchester Birds Do VDay'. VDay is a global campaign to stop violence against women and the brainchild of Eve Ensler, an American playwright and activist who penned *The Vagina Monologues.* Every year Eve allows charities and women's groups access to her script, stage direction and campaign material to stage their own performance of *The Monologues* with local women performing as a way of raising funds and awareness of violence against women. For the second year running I was in the thick of auditioning the cast, rehearsing, sourcing event sponsorship, selling tickets etc. and I also had to step in and take a performing role as one of our cast had dropped out at the last minute due to nerves! I did all of this on crutches in severe pain. At the same time I was delivering a 12-week Stardom intervention programme in Gloucester for a diverse group of 15 troubled and vulnerable girls. Some girls were in care, others already excluded from school etc. For the duration of this weekly programme I had to travel to Gloucester twice a week (400 mile round trip) and deliver a four-hour group session alongside coaching five of the girls over a two-month period.

For the duration of both these programmes I was in a wheelchair and on crutches and popping painkillers. What got me through was my emotional resilience, my support network, my awesome husband who drove me everywhere and looked after me, my top team at Girls Out Loud, my authenticity and my passion. Because I had already done the work on me to attract and embed all of this, when the crisis hit I could call on these resources fast. As authenticity is my number one value and a watch word by which I live, I had no fear in asking and accepting help, displaying my vulnerability, or being real.

The bottom line: do the work, do not go with the flow, it is passive and may feel like the safest option, but in the long run it gets you in hot water.

Repair the roof while the sun is shining!

LESSON TWO
I know for sure emotional resilience is the diet of champions

I believe emotional resilience is the secret weapon to endurance, it is a fundamental trait for success in any field. When the going gets tough the tough push on through, they do not quit. That pushing is resilience and as a society we do not seem to value it highly enough or recognise the route to embedding it. We avoid failure at all costs but without failure we cannot hone our resilience. If you never risk, you never fail and resilience eludes you. Nowhere is this more obvious than in our young.

ACADEMIC PROWESS IS NO SUBSTITUTE FOR EMOTIONAL RESILIENCE

Finally someone of note, Tanya Byron, a leading child psychologist has said what we at Girls Out Loud have been talking about for years: 'Risk-averse parents are damaging children.'

Byron is referring, in the main, to middle class parents who through a combination of pressure and protection create an environment of 'no failure here please' which in turn results in anxiety attacks, lack of emotional resilience and a 'play it safe' mentality.

I have seen this behaviour manifest in many academically bright teenage girls from 'good' families, in 'good' schools. They are in a permanent state of fear and worry about whether they are good enough, overly concerned about letting parents/ teachers down as they know for sure they must deliver excellent exam results and get into the best university, at a time when university is not necessarily 'one size fits all'.

One 17-year-old girl I spoke to recently was explaining how terrified she was of taking her driving test for fear of failing! Another one talked about how sad she was that music was her passion but she had to drop it as one of her subjects as she only achieved a B+ in her mocks and this was deemed unacceptable.

You don't have to be a professional to know this is not healthy. Whilst we don't want our children to fail, failing is often the best lesson, and a very powerful one at that. It is the only way to build emotional resilience as failing forces you to reflect, review and change.

Byron goes on to say the risk averse, litigious culture we are living in does nothing to help our children assess the dangers and risk of any given situation, and I agree. I think we wrap them up in so much cotton wool they struggle to breathe. Children no longer 'play out', create adventures or ride their bikes.

'Into the house children, there's a gentle breeze on the way!' AR-GHHHHHH!

Our education system is driven by targets and testing and this does not help. In reality this stops teachers being innovative or nurturing creativity in our children.

We need to rethink this and rethink it fast, we are seeing more and more teenagers in meltdown, with mental health issues, anxiety disorders and in general sad and confused. 12 A* GCSEs is NOT going to matter if they have so little confidence or belief in themselves they can barely leave the house!

Emotional resilience is the mark of a winner, it is character building, strength and an 'I can do' attitude all rolled into one. It is the greatest gift we can give ourselves and our children but it demands courage to embrace failure to get access to it and build the muscle.

LESSON THREE
I know for sure failure is a gift

I have failed often and spectacularly in my life. In fact sometimes I have repeated the same mistake over and over as I clearly did not get the lessons first time around! However, I would not give up these failures for a gold watch as this is where all my lessons have been revealed to me. I have learned everything I ever needed to know about business and life in the shadow of failure; in particular, in business, when I am flying high on success I very rarely learn anything new as I am too busy enjoying my success and spending the money! As I am a risk taker, my failures come thick and fast and I consider them part of the process of business. I am not talking about the 'game over' kind of failures, rather the 'OK, so that did not work' kind that encourages me to be better, try harder, work smarter. I also say being in business is like the first day in a new job every day – the market is unpredictable, customers are fickle, your art is unique and you have little intelligence on what is around the corner.

We still seem to carry a stigma about failing and in business we take it too personally. This needs to change. See previous habit about EMOTIONAL RESILIENCE! In the States you are not even considered an entrepreneur unless you have failed several times, and talk to any entrepreneur about their business journey, they will be as proud of their failures and their comeback to glory as any of their easy successes.

Failure is very rarely personal. It is a set of circumstances, some out of your control, others silly wrong turns but all coming together in a lesson to show you a different way, a better way. It is not the worst thing that can happen, the worst thing that can happen is not to risk or try in the first place. Fear of failure is crippling and in reality it is not the failing that matters, it is what you do next that separates the players from the spectators.

One of the frame-breaking mistakes I have repeated twice in business is overriding my intuition about partnerships. The first time I did this was back in 2006 when I agreed to go into business with my personal trainer to develop a social network/event company for discerning adults looking to meet like-minded people in the city. Kate and I were great friends but should never have become business partners. I knew this intuitively, but chose to override my niggles because I thought it would be fun and I loved spending time in her company. Not the basis for a successful business partnership. I was right; as the business gathered momentum we attracted an investor and the relationship fell to pieces. The investor refused to release the funds unless we shifted from a 50/50 partnership to a 60/40 in my favour due to my business acumen. At the time I thought this was reasonable as Kate had no business track record and he was protecting his investment. She felt differently and alongside trying to keep the investor on board I had to manage a very personal business break-up. Our friendship did not survive much to my regret, and the week before I was due to sign an agreement for a £1 million pound investment, the business angel decided to change the terms and I walked away, with nothing to show other than a sizeable debt and a lost friend. Frustrating as it seems I repeated this mistake a year later when I agreed to a partnership with another woman to create The Well Heeled Divas, only this time my potential partner and I hardly knew each other. I was at a low point, having just lost an opportunity of a lifetime and my vulnerability must have been palpable. I liked this woman and admired her gumption and her commitment to her own personal development was impressive, she had spent thousands on a range of courses and was ready to rock. Again my intuition was singing to me to take it slow and consider a different business structure, but we shared a high creator energy, so true to form we both jumped right in. The cracks appeared within a year as we both wanted to be in control and our ideas for the future of the business seemed to get further and further apart. By late 2008 we could hardly finish a conversation without it reducing to conflict, and despite spending a day with one of the UK's top business coaches to mediate a way forward, our relationship hit rock bottom and I found myself in another painful, personal and expensive business break-up.

In both these scenarios I ended up carrying the debt as I bought my partner's shares in order to maintain the brand, goodwill and current trading. On reflection I should have walked away from the first business when the partnership failed, but the second time the Diva business was attached to my core purpose as 90% of the intellectual property was my life's work. I also created the brand and the positioning and I knew this was an important moment. Taking total ownership allowed me to shift up several gears, readjust the messages to fit with my personal values and reignite my passion for the business again.

You will be pleased to know I have not and will not repeat this mistake again. I agree with the investor on partnerships; they are problematic and unless you know the individual very well and spend time up front setting out your stall and defining contract terms and exit plans they are risky affairs. Too often and too fast conflicts arise. l have seen the ugly demise of many family businesses. My learnings from these failures are around protection, contracts, having the difficult conversations and listening to my intuition. If it feels wrong or too rushed or uncomfortable I know I need to step back and review.

I know for sure I will continue to fail, I am a risk taker and an advocate of living an outstanding life. It goes with the territory!

LESSON FOUR
I know for sure change is personal

This may sound obvious but how many times have you tried to change someone else? Your kids, your friends, your work colleagues, your spouse/partner? We all tend to have a touch of 'the fixer' in us and even though our intentions are admirable, in reality you cannot change anyone else, you can only change you. But guess what? When you change, the people around you have to change anyway as your shift in behaviour or actions causes a shift in their response – bingo!

I see this all the time in my work and quite often come face to face with it in my own life. The only way you can help other people to change is if they ask for your help and this is where coaching and a variety of other external support comes in. Other than this you simply have to watch them live life on their terms however frustrating this is.

You can explain concepts, cause and effect, behaviours and outcomes. You can express your opinion and share your experience, but personal instructions and fixing are a no go.

Most of us expend a considerable amount of our precious time attempting to change other people – our partners, our kids, our boss, our employees, our family and friends. We want to mould them to our values and beliefs, to make them see the world the way we do, to encourage them that our way is best. We do not do this from a malicious or negative standpoint, we genuinely believe we are helping them to solve a problem or rise to a challenge, or do the right thing. But the right thing for who? If the decision is made with our back story, with our mindset, with our values and beliefs and with our view of the world, how can it possibly be the right decision for anyone else?

If we subscribe to the philosophy of individuality and the view that we are all unique human beings then how can our solution be fit for any other person than our self?

Science tells us that there is no such thing as objective reality, there is only our own reality. We see the world through a set of personal filters based on our experience only.

I am currently working through the frustration of not being able to help, or should I say fix, someone very close to me who is repeating some destructive behaviour patterns and as a result is unhappy, down and feeling stuck. It is kind of irrelevant that I can see some of the mistakes she is making, or that I know she is capable of so much more than she allows herself to believe, or that she is continually sabotaging her future as a form of protection, or that the patterns she repeats are grounded in self-hatred and fear. Until she gets this, until she learns to love herself, I am pretty powerless and can only stay close to her, hold her hand, let her know I care, tell her I am here for her and wait.

If I try to fix her or rescue her on my terms, or take away her decision-making ability, I deny her the emotional resilience she will gain from working through it and I also deny her the all-important life lessons she so needs to internalise to ensure that next time life throws her a low ball she does not fall over.

Even knowing this on an intellectual and emotional level does not make it any less painful to watch someone you love in distress, but I cannot change her without her permission, and even with permission, every professional bone in my body screams at me to step back.

So the next time you start a sentence with 'I know what you should do...' think on it, it is their life not yours, advice is always welcome, instructions less so.

As a coach and game-changer, it is my passion and purpose to create and empower personal change in others. But in my professional capacity my clients have given me permission to facilitate this journey gently, so my input is challenging but welcome. However, as far as everyone else is concerned my fixing and challenging is not quite as welcome and often I have to cover my mouth with duct tape and put myself in an emotional straight jacket just to stay silent and disassociated!

The only person you can fix is the one that looks back at you in the mirror every morning!

LESSON FIVE
*I know for sure the only person
responsible for your life is YOU*

The life you have today is a result of the decisions and life choices you made yesterday, last week, last month and a year ago. If you are unhappy with the harvest you need to step up, take responsibility and change what you sow. If all you ever do is blame everyone else for your life what does that make you? It's not my fault, it's my husband, my parents, the kids, my boss, my sister, my team, the bank, the Government, the education system, the media etc. etc. How does this help? How can you change anything if you are not in control of it? The only thing you are in control of is you! Once you get this, you will soar!

Blaming the world and his wife for your life makes you a victim and victims are weak, they are helpless and they have given away their power. Behaving as a victim is also pretty unattractive and will only ever attract more victims to your door. Now let's be clear about what I am saying here. I am not suggesting that you are always to blame when things don't work out the way you planned, but I am saying you will become a victim if you allow yourself to wallow and expect everyone else to fix it.

When my first life partner Geoff deceived me financially, as you recall I forgave him, came up with a survival plan and moved on. I did this not just because I loved him, but because I accepted some responsibility for the situation I now found myself in. Was I not as responsible for our finances as he? Hell yes, but I was too busy focused on my career and studies, I was in the final year of an MBA and had little time for anything other than work. 'All work and no play makes Jane a dull and dumb girl, eh!'

He was clearly struggling and I had not even noticed; I had simply devolved all financial responsibility to him including the roof over my head, my bank account, all the bills and insurances. When I think about this now it makes me shiver with foolishness. It would be easy to just blame him and say it was not my fault but I knew and felt otherwise.

The hardest lesson for me here was that he felt I had become unapproachable and he did not know how to tell me he was in trouble. Boy, that one hurt!

So I accepted some responsibility – not all, but I understood my role in the dance and we moved on. When he repeated this behaviour a few months later, now my responsibility was to take action and leave. Staying would be telling him it was OK to continue to disrespect me and I am all too aware that we teach people how to treat us.

I hear women talking about their men all the time in a way that assumes they have no responsibility for his behaviour, e.g. 'He always says this to me, or does this.' My response is always, 'No, ladies, you ALLOW him to treat you that way.' It is a slight change of language, but a world of difference in meaning.

Step up and be the creator of your own destiny, it is too precious to hand over to anyone else.

LESSON SIX

I know for sure you become who you mix with

Without doubt you become who you choose to hang around with – in fact, more than this, Anthony Robbins says you will never exceed the expectations of the five people you spend the most time with, so choose wisely, eh?

I define a peer as someone whose opinion you value, quite often this is not necessarily a lifelong friend or a family member. For instance, if you run your own business and need to bounce a few product ideas around and your parents have worked as employees all their life they may not be the best people to offer insight to your challenge. Or if you are an ambitious and bright professional woman looking for her first board appointment you may not get the advice or inspiration you need from your best friend who is a part-time dental hygienist with three kids under eight!

A peer is someone who inspires you, who is on the same journey as you and gets you. Got any?

I am passionate about connecting women and creating empowering peer groups. One of our key programmes at The Well Heeled Divas is a Diva Powerteam where I invite 12 dynamic women on a similar journey to connect, share and inspire each other as part of a structured mastermind circle. They meet four times a year and the power in the room is magical! I love them and have been facilitating them for over seven years. It is amazing what can happen when you connect sassy women and invite them to step up and show up for each other. Here are some Powerteamers sharing their experience:

"Within half an hour of our first Diva Powerteam meeting, I knew that it was going to be an incredible experience. Jane had brought together a group of women, all with challeng-

es to deal with and all with the desire to develop themselves and others. The energy in the room was fantastic – and my own personal self-belief increased measurably through the feedback and support, even at that first meeting. I would recommend that anyone who feels like their potential is lying dormant, and who wants a 'mastermind' team of supporters to help lift them to the next level/s, should definitely consider joining a Diva Powerteam with Jane Kenyon."

Nina Lockwood - Intuitive Interim & Executive Search

"Being part of Jane's Diva Mastermind group has been life changing. I had no idea it would be so useful to get outside perspective on my business from a group of intelligent business women. Jane is a master facilitator and an inspiration in what she achieves through her social and business ventures and her insights as a serial entrepreneur are priceless. I highly recommend Jane's Diva Powerteam."

Jane Barrett, Author and Founder of The Career Farm

So how hot are you then?

I challenge you to think about the thermometer test. Let's say your identity is like a thermometer and wherever the temperature gauge is, is where you live, e. g.74. Now if you attempt to make changes in your life, like get a better job, talk about having your own business, hook up with someone rich etc. and move up the scale to say 90, your peers will react. How they react depends on where they live on the scale. If they too are a 74 they will start to feel uncomfortable with your shift and try to sabotage you. They will question your motives and dissuade you from stepping up. They will tell you that you are becoming too big for your boots and try everything to get you back to 74, where they believe you belong. Now, they are not doing this out of malice, they are acting on fear of loss. They value you in their life and they are afraid of losing you but something else is going on too. Your talk of change, your need to step up is like holding a mirror up to their life too and quite often they do not like what they see. Now, the same group will also pick you up, support you and motivate you to get back to 74 if you fall below due to some critical moments and low times, but they will never lift you above 74.

Do you know where you live? Are you listening to your current peers and joining in the self-sabotage? Do you feel trapped in your current circle? Can you see how liberating and empowering it is to have a peer group around you who all want to hit 100 on the thermometer scale?

Let me share a story that drums home this lesson...

The farmyard was quiet one sunny Monday morning and to be honest the animals were all a tad bored so they got together and decided to have a singing competition to kill some time before the farmer arrived and the day got started. They appointed the pig as the judge and two key competitors stepped up: the crow and the bluebird. The crow won the toss and took his position on the largest tree branch in the yard, took a deep breath, opened his beak and started to sing – well, if you could call it singing. It was more like screeching and all the animals in the yard did their best to cover their ears with their paws, claws, hoofs and feet!

Thankfully, after a few minutes the crow ran out of steam and stepped back to make way for the only other contestant, the bluebird. The tiny, delicate and rather shy bluebird took his position, lifted his head and started to sing. The animals were mesmerised, his voice was like silk, his melodies were heaven sent and none of the animals wanted him to stop.

At the end of the show the pig announced the crow to be the winner and immediately the bluebird flew away and perched on the barn roof with tears falling down his face matting his beautiful feathers. The mother hen, the most caring of all the barn residents, approached him and said with love, 'Bluebird, please do not cry, it was only a silly competition, it is not worthy of your tears.' To which the bluebird replied, 'My dear mother hen I am not crying about the competition. I am just so disappointed I allowed myself to be judged by a pig!'

Think on, who are you allowing to judge you? Are they worthy of you?

LESSON SEVEN
*I know for sure self-belief and self-love
are the keys to a meaningful life*

These two are close bedfellows and the key differentiators when it comes to success in any field. Somehow we are all born with an abundance of both but as we mature they seem to be playing a permanent game of hide and seek with us! This tells me that they are sensitive to external influences and every experience we internalise has the ability to improve them or chip away at them.

Let's talk about self- belief

I know for sure that without steadfast self-belief the world of entrepreneurship is a scary place. It is a competitive, dynamic and relentless arena with very little recognition for a job well done and even fewer places to hide when it goes wrong. You do not only need absolute belief in your product and business, you need 100% belief in your ability to deliver it and deliver it at a profit. I am sure this is true of any leadership position too.

As someone who thinks in pictures, I see my self-belief like one of those huge liquid vats you see on game shows with a measure up the side, and every time I push myself beyond my comfort zone and succeed the vat gets filled with liquid, in varying quantities dependent on the level of the success and courage I expound. So, for instance, if I delivered a great keynote which was well received by the organisation that employed me and had an impact on the audience, I will see the measure rise slightly as this is my day job! However, if I secure an above average contract or sponsorship deal for Girls Out Loud, the liquid measure will rise higher. However, the bad news is the liquid in this vat can also reduce when I beat myself up for not being perfect or when I fail to see an opportunity or close a deal, or I overreact to a throwaway comment because I am overtired etc.

I know my self-belief is a moving target that demands continuous investment. It can only be as strong and resilient as I am.

The world of personal development is teeming with tools, techniques, books and programmes aimed at improving your self-belief, so do them all! It really is a habit and anything that helps hone a habit is a good idea as far as I am concerned but find some techniques that work for you. I am a fan of mantras, keeping a gratitude journal, surrounding myself with winners, controlling my emotional state via anchors, watching TED talks, positive thinking and visualisation, but I am also a huge reader and never stop investing in my personal development, attending seminars and retreats on a regular basis to feed my mindset, catch any negativity before it has a chance to stick and meet like-minded winners.

Let's talk about self-love

During the past 20 years I cannot tell you how many women and teenage girls I have coached on the subject of self-love. The best romance of them all but the toughest to surrender to. For women in particular this is so tied up in the way we look. Here is a blog I wrote on this recently:

Mirror, mirror on the wall – why our reflection is killing our self-esteem...

Pick up any glossy magazine on any day of the week and by the time you have turned the last page you can be forgiven for feeling a little inadequate. The airbrushed images and messages simply support our unrealistic goals of perfection. The messages are powerful and very subliminal. If you brought your attention to the content once in a while, it's likely even after a cursory glance you will be thinking:

- My hair is not long or thick enough

- My nails are not strong or long enough

- My lashes are not full enough

- My stomach's not flat enough

- My teeth are not white enough

- My skin is not smooth enough

- My skin is the wrong colour

- My nose is the wrong shape

- My lips are not full enough

- My boobs are too small and not pert enough

- I have too much cellulite

- I am the wrong size, shape, weight and my silhouette is all wrong!

Add to this the pressure to lose your baby weight within weeks, be a yummy mummy, a vixen at work, a siren at home, a well-balanced career girl with domestic goddess tendencies, and a supermum and it is not difficult to understand why so many of us are in the throes of an all-out identity crisis permanently! When did we buy into the media hype that we are not enough?

If we do not love ourselves, how do we expect men to? They are bemused by our body battering. They want our feminine curves, our soft bodies, our vulnerabilities. Quite often they feel powerless to convince us of this. They don't care if we have a tummy or cellulite (most would not even be able to point to this if their life depended on it!); they would not even notice if we put on a few pounds, or stone in some cases, and I challenge you to evoke even a millisecond of recognition on the subject of orange peel skin!

What we interpret as imperfections men cherish as our uniqueness and our vulnerability. They don't want to change this, they love this. They know it is unreal and impossible to look like a supermodel, their logic and common sense tells them this is fake – even the supermodels don't look like the magazine covers in the flesh. They care not a jot about this. And maybe, just maybe they feel threatened by all this talk of perfection, because it may be their turn next? If you demand perfection in all things, what does that say about you? How come they can see that the models are fake yet we refuse to believe?

Our body hang-ups are ours and ours alone. If we hate looking in the mirror and can say nothing positive about our reflection, then we are simply chipping away at our self-esteem and how can we be role models for our daughters with self-hatred screaming back at us? We need to step up and own this issue. We need to find our courage, our voice and inner strength to stop disfiguring our authenticity and stop feeding our insecurities with hate, drugs, surgery, addictions, obsessions, diseases and self-flagellation. We need to recognise our greatness and know that we are so much more than what we weigh or what we look like.

Believe me when I say you are not alone in coming to terms with this identity crisis. It is shameful it is global and it is crippling the self-esteem of our young girls every day.

Barbie doll beauty generation – stuff you don't want to hear...

The pressure to conform to the Barbie doll beauty ideal has been fuelled by the beauty industry for decades, but now, particularly in the past 10 years as we have welcomed images of women as portrayed in porn as empowering and the sex industry has gone mainstream, a more serious, aggressive player has entered the market for our hearts and souls: cosmetic surgery. From Botox to total body lifts we are bombarded by adverts telling us we really can be perfect, it's a modern day miracle and our right! All of this is simply escalating our body hatred but with our permission, or so it seems to me. We talk about lap dancing, pole dancing and Burlesque as being empowering, we idolise celebrities, glamour models and porn stars and we belittle and insult professional women and bully young girls who refuse to buy into this 'doll like' version of beauty. Whatever happened to sisterhood?

Now, don't get me wrong, I am all for a little enhancement, I see nothing wrong in working with what you've got, but this need to reinvent and distort our natural beauty beyond make-up and traditional female adornments is a little worrying and cannot be sending positive messages to our young girls.

My message: stay authentic, know who you are and what is important to you. Be strong, be kind, be bold, be beautiful, in fact just be YOU, because YOU are enough exactly as you are.

Unfortunately this lack of self-love is not just affecting our identity, it can destroy our relationships too. I will never forget what a wise man, Peter, a fellow student on my MBA programme said to me back in 1992. He saw me saying goodbye to my life partner Geoff at the airport as we were Barcelona bound on a university exchange trip. He surmised there were some issues going on in the relationship by the way I was a tad distant and dismissive towards Geoff and desperate to get away and yet he was fawning all over me and reluctant to leave. So as I re-joined the check-in queue, Peter turned to me and said, 'You know Jane, until you fall in love with you, you will never be capable of loving anyone else.' I thought this was profound and at the time he was spot on. I felt Geoff was suffocating me and I hated myself for how I was treating him but the issues were definitely deeper and Peter's words hit a nerve.

Twenty-two years later and I cannot tell you how many times I have had this conversation with other people. A lack of self-love is a relationship killer, here's how...

When you do not love you, when you are less than pleased by your reflection and/or your identity and achievements etc. you find it hard to accept that anyone else could possible love you so evoke one of two strategies to make yourself feel better:

1. You settle for less than you deserve. You play safe, you aim low and you accept very little in the way of adoration, support, attention and love because you don't think you deserve it anyway. This can result in some pretty destructive relationships, even abusive ones as you have so little self-respect you are numb to what is on offer.

2. You continually punish those who do love you because it seems so false. How can they possible love YOU? This punishment takes the form of permanent testing. So how much do you love me? If you loved me you would... If you really loved me you would... Eventually the partner in this relationship becomes weary and gives up. There are only so many times they can say and prove to you they love you. If you don't believe it they are powerless.

Both these scenarios are so heartbreaking and so unnecessary. It is your job to fall in love with you. To find your inner light, to celebrate your uniqueness, to laugh at your foibles, to discover your charm and wit, to be proud of your vulnerabilities and to shout about your successes. And when you find someone who falls in love with you too, go with it and surrender to the process.

'I am selfish, impatient and a little insecure. I make mistakes, I am out of control and at times hard to handle. But if you can't handle me at my worst then you sure as hell don't deserve me at my best.'

Marilyn Monroe

LESSON EIGHT
I know for sure self-awareness is peace

Many things I have mentioned so far in this section may still be a mystery to you – your identity, your values, your beliefs, emotional resilience, victim complex, self-love and so on. I cannot tell you how liberating it is to really know yourself. I mean really, really know yourself at your core. To know is to love and your journey is absolutely personal. The more you understand you, the faster you can react, the better your life choices, the easier it is to make decisions, attract the right people and find peace.

I challenge you find your truth and hold on to it, no matter what.

THERE IS A TIME FOR SILENCE AND A TIME TO BE HEARD

The people I admire most in life are those brave enough to step up and speak their truth. People like Maya Angelou, Seth Godin, Caitlin Moran, Russell Brand, Oprah and Jamie Oliver. Even when I am not in full agreement with their opinion I still admire their conviction and courage to stand up for their beliefs, so long as their view on life does not incite violence, oppression or injustice.

Too many of us spend our life searching for our voice but then seem far too quick to surrender it if someone dares to question us or we are asked to defend it. The minute any dissonance appears we step back and disappear.

Nowhere is this more prevalent than on social media where people openly share their views, opinions and likes, only to retract them swiftly if too many people disagree or question them. Why is this?

I find sheep-like behaviour depressing. I am more than happy to follow a leader if they have earned my respect, inspire me and have something to say that I can believe in, but too many people stay small and insignificant for fear of not being liked or being seen as too demanding or radical.

This kind of thinking is limiting and lame and has to go. My message is simple. Stand up and be heard, do not be afraid to speak your truth, own it and surrender it for no one! Your voice is unique, peerless and present. Use it or lose it!

Time spent getting to know you is time well spent. Write your story so far and see the lessons jump off the page; do the work to uncover your values and passions and celebrate your unique take on life!

LESSON NINE

*I know for sure events are just emotions
waiting to be acknowledged*

I have done enough personal development courses and NLP training to know there is no such thing as an event, there is only the emotion we attach to it long after the event is forgotten. It is the emotion we remember and absorb into our identity and story. We have a tendency to extract key emotions from every situation that are already in line with our existing beliefs, positive or negative, so if we already have a limiting belief that resides in our subconscious screaming 'you are not bright enough to secure a director level appointment' then every significant event related to this belief that does NOT result in a positive outcome feeds this belief. Every time an event does not turn out perfectly we have a choice to own the negative or positive emotions from it. Does that make sense? Our subconscious mind is surrounded by a huge filter and we decide what we are going to let in and what we are going to disregard. We refer to this as a self-fulfilling prophecy and it works like a dream!

If we believe we are not enough, everything that happens to us proves this in some way, because we change the meaning of it until it does!

But guess what? Using an amazing NLP coaching technique called reframing we can change the meanings/emotions of events in our past by reframing them from a negative to a positive. Now I know this sounds too good to be true, but I have done it many times personally and facilitated this process for hundreds of clients over the years so I know its power.

Let me share an example from my story.

Remember the traumatic night I was cast aside by my father, the man I idolised and adored? Do you think I may have attached some pretty destructive emotions to that event? Here was the most important male adult in my life to date, banishing me in the most dismissive and cruel way ever. Do you think maybe I internalised some negative emotions about me as a result? Here is a potential list of negative emotions my subconscious could have played with at the time:

NEGATIVE:

- This is the most important man in my life, if he can fall out of love with me in an instant, I am clearly unlovable and not worthy of love.

- All the men that love me will eventually tire of me and desert me.

- Clearly my presence and personality upsets women of a certain age and background.

- I am a disappointment on many levels.

- I have been abandoned and this is my fault, but I do not know why, so until I do I will keep repeating this.

- I am meant to be alone.

- My father chose someone else over me. I am not good enough.

- I deserve to be alone.

Now, what I know for sure is there are also lots of positive emotions I could just as easily have absorbed from the same event too, but I think the mind disregards them in favour of the negative, when the negative shouts louder. When we reframe an event the key is to reinstate the positive with the added benefit of hindsight. So here are some positive emotions from the same event:

POSITIVE:

- This environment is toxic and stopping me from shining.

- My relationship with my father is unhealthy and damaging my spirit.

- I embrace my freedom.

- I accept the gift of emotional resilience that will be the foundation for my amazing journey.

- This event will be my defining moment – it will be the making of me and set me on a very different path. One I will never be allowed or encouraged to pursue if I remain caged as my father's princess.

Amazing that all of these emotions were hidden, eh? My first encounter with personal development, apart from reading, was when I was 29 and I enrolled on The Journey weekend with Brandon Bays – 13 years after THE event! It was during this process Brandon helped me to finally get closure by reframing this moment in my life. It was the most liberating experience, never to be surpassed on any other course I have done since and believe me there have been many! I was ready for change; this is important, until you are ready all attempts at reframing will fail. I was aware that I needed to deal with my father issues, I was unable to grieve for something I had lost and I am sure this was the reason I became ill. I felt strong and independent but Geoff telling me he felt I was unapproachable had hurt me at a deep level and I wondered if I was subconsciously not letting him in, for fear of being rejected all over again. I was fed up of feeling angry. I was ready.

Brandon helped me see all the positives around my story, the love, the good intentions and the misgivings. This process was both painful and empowering. I may have sailed through this trauma in my twenties and appeared confident, indestructible and in control, but in reality this was not what was going on in my head or my heart. I had blocked the grief, channelled it elsewhere. I was in denial and when I released it, really felt it, surrendered to it, I started to grieve and the true healing process began. I can remember crying from Friday evening to Sunday evening and by Monday morning I felt drugged I was so exhausted yet I had a sense of calm and lightness.

So, the reframe... All the work I did on this weekend allowed me to dump my negative emotional baggage and negative beliefs with regard to that fateful evening. I now believe, wholeheartedly, my father made the right decision choosing me on that night. He knew I would survive, he knew for sure I was tough and I would be OK. He had just watched me survive one of the toughest schools and come out on top socially, even though academically I failed. He knew I was a resilient young woman with the means to take care of myself both emotionally and financially, and when faced with a choice of losing his wife, who was totally dependent on him (by his choice) and the mother to his other two children and the orchestrator of his home life, or his high-spirited, street-smart little princess, the choice was obvious. In doing this he set me free to live life on my own terms, to define my own success and to step out from his shadow.

Now, I know you might think he has got off scot free here and as a parent his behaviour was unacceptable and he should know better, but should he? How? We only learn to parent through our own experience and we tend to inherit the values of our parents along the way. I knew very little about my parents' background, except that they both came from poor families with many emotional hang-ups and in my mother's case a severe lack of love and/or emotional connection. I understood why my father would place so much importance on money and materialism when he had nothing and I also understood why both of them found it hard to express emotion or show love. My father's way of showing love was always and has remained focused on money; my mother had her moments but they were few and far between and I know her demons must have impacted her life choices and behaviours along the way.

So, the bottom line – I forgave them both. To be fair, I had already forgiven my mother many years earlier when I understood her pain, her frustrations, the cause of her jealousy and the horrors of her childhood. I truly believe forgiveness gives you power and this reframe was possibly the most important part of my personal development journey.

Let me leave you with this classic: everyone does the best they can do, with the resources available to them at, the time.

LESSON TEN

I know for sure authenticity is the Holy Grail,
the end game

For me this is the thing we are all striving for. It is the road we end up on as we assimilate the other nine habits into our life. It is about finding your voice, defining your personal brand and feeling comfortable with the V word – oh yes VULNERABLI-TY! Easy then, eh?

The whole notion of authenticity fascinates me. Everyone seems to crave it, talk about it and own it but very few people truly live their life with it front and centre. It has become a bit of a fad word, hijacked by the personal development/spirituality industry and thus normalised when it is anything but normal!

I subscribe to authenticity in all things. It is my watch word, my number one value and above all else my END GAME.

I believe it is at the heart of all personal development and growth. To be authentic is to be real, to be true, to be YOU. This is why I call it the end game, because most of us spend a lifetime trying to find the courage to let go of our fake and 'public' masks, alongside hiding our true emotions so we will be liked and not upset anyone.

So why is it so hard to do?

- Being true to you means you sometimes have to upset others by saying no or disagreeing or opting to go your own way.

- Being true to you means accepting you are not perfect, learning to fail with flair and making mistakes by the bucket load.

107

- Being true to you means owning your weaknesses and flaws.

- Being true to you means not worrying about what other people think ALL the time.

- Being true to you means working on you, keeping your ego in check and being self-aware.

- Being true to you means letting go of the need to be perfect inside and out.

- Being true to you means sometimes embracing your vulnerability and being OK with that. Yikes! Really?

Phew, no wonder this stuff is tough!

I was reminded how tough recently when I was working with a group of disengaged, disruptive, under-achieving, vulnerable and very tough teenage girls at an inner city school.

After nine weeks of rapport building, nurturing and absolute support their behaviour towards me on one day was particularly venomous. I gave them every benefit of the doubt, changed my approach, language, tonality, body language and material but to no avail. At this point I felt the only thing left in my kitbag was to put my vulnerability on the table. I explained, gently and without judgement, how upset and hurt I felt by their behaviour and the only reason I put up with it was because I genuinely cared about them and wanted to see them shine and create a life of possibilities. I then put my hands up and admitted I was at a loss as to what to do next and sat in silence.

This created a serious pattern break in the room. The girls sat in shocked silence for a few moments then we all reconnected on a deeper level – we had tears, apologies and hugs and then the group dynamic changed and we moved on.

This was not easy for me to do. I had to hold on to my courage and share my vulnerability on an emotional level without really knowing the next step. It felt risky and liberating all at the same time.

This is the reality of being authentic. The outcome is unknown but what I know for sure is you can only be you; refusal to claim your authenticity for fear of being rejected, or failing, or being alone or any other fear is a fake life and one not worthy of you.

In the words of Brene Brown, my ultimate guru on vulnerability:

'Let go of who you think you are supposed to be and embrace who you are. When we numb the dark, we also numb the light. You cannot be selective on which emotions you share, share them all and connect wholeheartedly.'

This scary word vulnerability shows up in so many of our stories. I am such a people watcher and tend to eavesdrop unintentionally on conversations in bars and coffee shops while I am waiting for people all the time. It provides me with great material, and here is one such occasion.

Are we scared of love?

This week I was sitting in my local wine bar waiting for a friend and overheard three 40-something professional women talking about their relationships. 'Well what John has taught me is what I don't want in a relationship – I don't want a full-on relationship, lots of attention or marriage. I am more than happy with dinner a few nights a week and the occasional sex.' Really? Seriously, is this the definition of a modern day relationship demanded by today's professional busy woman?

Oh God I hope not! What happened to love, to hopeless, all-out infatuation when you simply cannot live without him and miss him even if you spend a few days apart? Or is this me? Am I a dated, old-fashioned Disney romantic?

Or is something else going on here? Is our reluctance to let go, risk and allow love in another symptom of fear? Are we suppressing our vulnerability as a form of self-protection and control?

Sometimes love hurts; sometimes it does not work out; sometimes he cheats and you walk; sometimes you cheat and he walks; sometimes it becomes boring or family scenarios make it impossible to settle, but and it's a BIG but, if the alternative to seeking love is dinner a couple of times a week with the occasional romp I will take bliss, however temporary it may be any day!

Back to the guru on this subject, Brene Brown. She defines vulnerability as connection, what gives purpose to life, why we are here, and whilst some people embrace it others stay in ignorance and denial. People who embrace it have the courage, compassion and connection to tell their story of who they are with their whole heart, brave enough to be flawed and share their flaws with others.

Those that ignore it do so in several ways:

1. They numb it by addiction, medication, obesity.

2. They make the uncertain certain and attempt to eradicate any discourse from their life. Everything is black and white, yes or no, do or don't.

3. They attempt to perfect – themselves, their kids and their environment.

4. They pretend that what they do does not have an effect on others.

I see at least 2, 3 and 4 showing up in this opening story, do you? Love has no certainty, you will only attract what you are prepared to give and every action has a reaction.

We must stop seeing vulnerability as a weakness as it is key to our authenticity and our story. A life where we take no risks is no life at all, unless you are aiming for mediocrity. People deserve to see all of you, flaws and all, because as you attempt to numb the pain you also numb the joy.

Personally...

Personally, I am not convinced we get this. We bandy this word around rather a lot but are we really subscribing to it? If being authentic is being real I have been vilified for this behaviour many times in my life.

To be truly authentic is to live our own truth, embrace our vulnerability, dump our external people-pleaser mentality and stand up for who we are and what we believe. But how often do we sabotage this to be liked? To be nice? To be fair? To conform?

And moreover, we are not exactly big fans of women who display authenticity unless it is our version of authenticity. If their behaviour does not align to our beliefs and values we are quick to criticise or distance ourselves from them. The way the nation responded to the passing of Maggie Thatcher was a case in point. And another recent display was the personal attack on Sheryl Sandberg on the release of her book *Lean In*.

Real is what's real for you, it is personal and certainly not universal. However, I know for most people the road to authenticity is a life's work. It certainly is for me. Many times I have readjusted my voice and power to make others feel more comfortable and then ended up feeling fake and stressed. The journey to self-love and acceptance is littered with lessons and revelations. But what I know for sure is that every time I sidestep my authenticity I feel the burn!

Confidence to be you, regardless of your environment, is true empowerment and the only way to live an authentic life. Constantly comparing your life, your skillset, your values and your achievements to others is fruitless and leads to life envy – the most negative energy on the planet.

Realigning your behaviour to meet other people's expectations is exhausting and NOT sustainable. So step up and be proud to be you in your full Technicolor glory. Embrace the Girls Out Loud mantra…

To conclude

Be bold, be brave, be beautiful but most importantly be you. Because you are already enough and absolutely perfect just the way you are.

PART THREE
STEP ASIDE BRANSON
THE DIVAPRENEURS
ARE COMING!

'We are all creators, it's just some of us find the courage to share our creations with the world.'

INTRODUCTION

I have been an entrepreneur for over 20 years, and despite the financial roller coaster and several spectacular failures, I remain passionate about business and in particular working with women. Although many of the lessons and learnings in this section are gender wide I make no apologies for homing in on the unique female perspective of creating and leading businesses. It is where my heart is. However, over the past few years I have watched so many people in my entrepreneurial network walk away from their business and return to full-time employment. Why? No doubt the economy is tough and in tough times competition intensifies, banks stop lending and customers become more discerning. Clearly this all has a negative impact on cash flow but survival is about more than money in and money out. If you genuinely love what you are doing, have an unwavering passion for it and have burned all the bridges behind you, you can learn to live on less in the short term to stay in the game in the long term.

As a serial entrepreneur who has ridden the wealth to near bankruptcy roller coaster several times over the past 20 years I know more than most how important mindset is to success and sustainability in business. In fact, I would go as far as to say it is the key differential between endurance and quitting.

If pushed, here are my top five musts for business longevity:

1. SELF BELIEF – You must have this in bucketloads, not only to assuage the odd personal wobble but to fight off all the naysayers, dream thieves and disloyal customers! You must also have resilience and steadfast belief in your business concept/idea and your ability to deliver it on time, every time. If you do not believe you are the best and/or your solution is unique why should anyone else get excited about it?

2. SOUND PEER GROUP – We all need to be surrounded by people who get us, inspire us, support us and cheer for us even on the days when it all seems to be going pear shaped. In fact, particularly on those days! However, do not confuse peers with friends. A peer is someone whose opinion you value, who is in the same/ similar game, who is where you want to be or on the same journey etc. This does not always describe your friends, and whilst they are important, sometimes their opinion is not particularly insightful or helpful.

3. TENACITY/CAN DO ATTITUDE – The belief that potential is infinite is a given for an entrepreneur, tell me it can't be done and I will rise to the challenge! You need to have faith in your idea. If it is about changing the current market you may need to try several times to gain momentum; leverage takes time and obstacles will keep appearing. This is business as usual, and without dogged determination walking away is easy.

4. PASSION/PURPOSE – To stay in the business for the long haul you must be driven by something more than money. The need to make a difference is strong in most entrepreneurs, in fact this may be the reason they stepped up in the first place. Passion is contagious and when it oozes from your business brand and philosophy you are on your way to something sustainable.

5. BE IN FLOW – Attempting to be all things to all people is a recipe for disaster and demotivation. Know what flow means to you. Flow is what you do naturally, brilliantly – this could be selling and creating attraction to your business; leading the team; creating the back office automation or managing projects. If you are not in flow and enjoying the journey chances are no one else around you is in flow either and pretty soon it all starts

to feel like hard work. Know your value and delegate the rest.

So, to conclude, if you are not particularly juiced by what you are doing and why you are doing it, if you have no raving fans around you cheering you on and you don't really believe you are capable of succeeding anyway, the obvious option is to walk away. There is no point beating yourself up about this – the timing might not be right, the idea may need more work or you may need to work on your mindset – all doable!

The ultimate business philosophy is to build a business aligned to your passion and be in flow doing it.

The following section is my learnings and observations over the past 10 years of working with female entrepreneurs and the industry that supports them.

LESSON ONE
I know for sure entrepreneurship is all about mindset

You can have a business plan that makes your bank manager salivate, a fantastic recession-proof product and money in the bank, but without the right mindset to deliver and sustain this you will still fail and fail fast.

I still maintain that entrepreneurship is learnt behaviour and anyone with the right mindset can be a success, but let's just agree on what an entrepreneur is. My definition is someone who is building a business that is bigger than them; it has some leverage and the ability to make money without them. Not necessarily without them at the helm long term but certainly in the short term. It must also have some brand power and sustainability and be worth something in the long term to create a rewarding exit. It is not necessarily about empire building or employing hundreds of people or owning acres of real estate. Business has changed beyond recognition over the past 10 years, fortunes can now be made from your front room with a connection to millions of customers on your iPhone, but the desire and attitude remain the same.

I have motivated and coached thousands of women through my Divapreneur programme and the first thing we define and embed is:

THE DIVAPRENEUR MINDSET

DIVA – A business Diva is a sassy, strong role model who knows who she is, knows what she wants, is aligned with her passion and purpose, leads via her values, thinks big and is motivated by creating sustainable wealth in order to give back.

INFINITE POTENTIAL RULES – In my view, this is one of the key differentiators between workers and leaders. Leaders have a steadfast belief that potential is infinite and a serious 'can do' attitude. If you tell them something is impossible you will motivate them no end! Can you imagine the day Richard Branson presented his plans to his board to extend the Virgin brand to include commercial space travel? Would love to have been a fly on the wall on that day! Divapreneurs will find a way, they will make it happen, they will keep the faith, they have gumption!

VISIONARY AND A BIG PICTURE THINKER – Divapreneurs start with the end in mind, they project a business that has potential beyond self-employment, they are not driven by the need to create a job, they are motivated by creating a business.

ACTION ORIENTATED – Divapreneurs are in the game, living it, believing it and taking massive action every day to endure. They recognise business is full of spectators who sit on the sidelines to watch, criticise and simply make a lot of noise, and players who are giving it their all on the pitch. Divaprenuers are players, in the game, full on and enjoying the process.

PEER NETWORK IN PLACE – Divapreneurs know the importance of a sound network, not just other entrepreneurs but advisors, mentors, financial supporters and other professional aides. They are more than likely to secure a business coach to keep them on track and accountable and will surround themselves with winners and dream makers not dream thieves.

RISK TAKER – Divapreneurs recognise risk is essential to grow a business but are not reckless. They recognise the only way to reduce risk is to gather information before taking the big decisions and they are steadfast in this regard. They step into their ideas, commit to them, defend them and burn all bridges behind them to ensure total immersion.

EXCITED ABOUT THE BUSINESS – Divapreneurs are excited about their business as it is aligned to their passion, purpose and values. This passion is contagious and allows buy-in from employees, customers, suppliers and advocates and they are clearly focused on the why not the what. What buys you a transaction, why gets you a brand and a tribe!

NEED TO MAKE A DIFFERENCE – Divapreneurs are driven by the need to make a difference, this picks up the why above. They are motivated by doing something bigger, better or different from what is already in the market. They may have a cause, a passion or an ambition to leave a legacy. One thing is for sure: when you meet them you will be left in no doubt as to why they do what they do and what is driving them.

ENHANCING THEIR OFFER ALL THE TIME – Divapreneurs stay close to their customers, recognise change is permanent and business is continually evolving and know that this impacts their offer. They are not complacent and this ensures they remain competitive.

UNDERSTAND LEVERAGE AND SUSTAINABILITY – Divapreneurs are driven by the need to build something bigger than them, they understand flow, have a long-term strategy for growth and are ready to let go of their emotional attachment.

RECOGNISED AS A LEADER – Divapreneurs do not necessarily follow the crowd, they head up a tribe and refuse to compromise on their values and/or voice.

SELF-BELIEF – Divapreneurs are resilient, get back up when knocked, stay in positive vibrations, have absolute belief in their business idea and their own abilities to deliver it and do not recognise failure as anything other than feedback and an opportunity to learn.

Phew eh? Can you see why this stuff takes a lifetime to master? It is a movable feast, but a sound plan and believe me when I say none of it happens by luck. Here's my view on luck.

HOW LUCKY ARE YOU?

I do get frustrated when people overuse the word lucky to justify or validate someone else's life choices and business success.

It is easy and guilt free to disregard someone else's hard work, risk, courage, tenacity, focus, resilience, passion, creativity and commitment as simply luck. Maybe it makes you feel better for your lack of gumption, but as someone who has spent thousands of pounds and many, many hours on my own personal development, I know for sure that any success I have attracted into my life has very little to do with luck.

To this end I would like to reframe this word from a passive, intangible, ethereal, hands-off concept that just appears to work like magic to a more realistic, action-orientated personal philosophy.

You see, I believe luck is a result of personal choices. We create it. It doesn't just happen to us, it happens as a direct result of what we do. In my world...

L stands for LOCATION

Location is about being in the right place at the right time. This can sometimes take months or years to get right but when it happens it feels like serendipity. Do not be fooled; knowing where the game is played is a strategy, demanding a clear niche, research, customer interaction and quite often market information only possible to glean through several failed attempts.

U stands for UNDERSTANDING

Identifying the right location is only the beginning; you kind of have to know what to do when you get there! The market very rarely issues instructions so you have to learn how the game works, how the market sings and who else is in it.

C stands for CONNECTIONS

And so we arrive at the people crossroads. So now you know where the game is played and how it is played. Time to make sure you have the right people on your team and in your network to actually play! Have you got a dream team? Are you surrounded by positive dream makers or negative dream thieves? Is your network proactive or asleep? Who is on your side?

K stands for KNOWLEDGE

The bad news is you only gain knowledge by doing, but the good news is every time you take action you learn; even if you fail to manifest the perfect results you have still gained valuable knowledge about the game. In business, practice makes near perfect, sitting back and simply watching, waiting and hoping for the magic to happen creates complacency and mediocrity and is a sure-fire way to quit rather than fail with lessons.

We have all heard the famous quote: 'The more I practise, the luckier I become.'

This interpretation of LUCK allows us to become more pro-active and responsible for our own destiny. It encourages momentum and encourages us to build emotional resilience – necessary traits for success, in my book.

So ask me if I am lucky? Hell yes, are you?

LESSON TWO

I know for sure when women grasp the entrepreneurial baton the game will change

I was recently part of a panel at a women's enterprise event and asked what holds women back in business.

Firstly let me say there has never been a better time to be a woman – we are at the peak of our emotional development, the UK has more female millionaires than ever before, the corporate world of leadership is starting to crack open and women are starting businesses at a healthy rate, leading the economic recovery; however, I would like to focus on female entrepreneurship. Now remember the definition of an entrepreneur in my book is someone building a business that is bigger than them, as opposed to self-employment which generally creates a job. We are pretty good at creating our own jobs, self-employment for women is growing at an alarming rate but I remain unconvinced this is because all these women are driven to build a business. It is more likely a smokescreen for financially crippling childcare costs, inflexible working hours and a testosterone-fuelled corporate sector that devalues feminine wisdom – but more about this later! Self-employment is the natural first step for most entrepreneurs, me included, but taking the next step to growth seems to be fraught with anxiety, fear and one too many obstacles for many. These obstacles are nothing to do with our capability and everything to do with our mindset. I have coached and mentored hundreds of women in business and some pretty clear trends have become apparent.

OUR NEED FOR PERFECTION IS STIFLING US. We need more qualifications, a better website, more twitter followers, more research and a knockout brand before we even dip our toe in the water. I cannot tell you how many times I have had this conversation: 'I am just not ready to take the next step yet. My website needs some work.' OK, I say, so when? And the reply: 'Well we are on the fifth version now so hopefully this year.' Arrrrgh!!! It will never be perfect, perfect does not exist. My mantra: **GET GOING and GET BETTER.** The market cannot respond to what you are planning, it can only respond to what you put out there. To learn to swim you must first get in the pool! Just JUMP!

WE ARE TOO EMOTIONALLY ATTACHED TO LET GO. A close ally of perfectionism is control. We believe no one can do all the work as well as us so we struggle to let go of ANYTHING. We talk about not being able to find the staff, how it is easier to just do it ourselves, but this is exhausting and hampers any growth. This is all about our emotional attachment to our business. I hear women refer to their business as their 'baby' all the time and with this goes a reluctance and in some instances real fear of letting go or allowing anyone else to look after their baby. We need to reframe this if we are to take our rightful place in the world of business. This control is all part of the superwoman cape we wear with pride that needs to go and is discussed in the next section. We will not grow businesses without some external investment, a management team, board of non-execs etc. We could easily apply the baby analogy but in a different way. Recognising that babies grow into children, teenagers then adults, and along the way we as parents need to step back and let them make some of the decisions to build resilience and gain an element of independence. Bingo! Think about your 'business baby' like this and we could be on to a winner!

WE ARE FINANCIALLY FEARFUL. One of the key fears most women hold on to is the fear of debt and they associate growing a business with getting into debt so they stay small and attempt to grow incrementally via their cash flow. In exceptional circumstances this can work but in most cases growth demands some form of financial investment and this is interpreted as debt so it is bad. I am fascinated by this association as we do not do it with other capital investments. If I asked a group of women to raise their hand if they own their own home, most of the room would be ablaze with proud, outstretched arms but the next question 'How many of you have a mortgage on this property?' shows me a very different picture. You see, you do not own your home if it is mortgaged. Stop your mortgage payments for six months and you will find out who owns your house! Yet we are comfortable with this debt, are we not? So could we not reframe financial debt to be an investment in our next 25-year future? Just a thought!

Also do not forget financial institutions feed this insecurity by being far more cautious lending to women, hence why we are seeing a growth in female-led investment funds and business angels. I can fill a chapter on the stories women have told me about the inappropriate questions bank managers have asked them when they have asked for a loan or the impossible criteria requested for an overdraft – and no, this is not the result of a tough economy when the same questions are not asked of men! Several times over my entrepreneurial career I have found it easier to secure a £1m investment than get a £5k overdraft.

WE ARE RELUCTANT TO TAKE OWNERSHIP OF SUCCESS AND SHUN RECOGNITION. The conversation opener goes like this: 'Well, I do not want to build an empire, I just want to provide a good life for my family.' As if building an empire is somehow unfeminine and distasteful and money a nasty word. It is true that women are more driven by values than hard cash but we are kidding ourselves if we do not think financial reward is OK for a job well done. The battle for our emancipation was founded on financial independence, and self-employment offers very little security in the long run.

What's wrong with growing a big business? Something to pass on to your kids as opposed to a measure to keep them? And why are we so shy when it comes to recognition? 'Oh it was nothing to do with me, I was just in the right place at the right time.' Ermmm YES clever you! Or 'Oh no it was a team effort, I had very little to do with it.' Duh! Who employed the team then? Own it! How can we encourage the next generation if we are constantly apologising for our success?

One of the issues I had as I started to move beyond self-employment was a fear of disconnection. I had a limiting belief that if it all got too big my personality would be marginalised and I would lose the customer interaction I so craved, as the business became more about the numbers and the transactions than my passion to change lives. Understanding my wealth profile and my value to my business helped me get perspective on this. Coming up later!

WE DON'T BELIEVE WE HAVE THE RIGHT SKILLSET.
Are you kidding? Business today is about connection, making a difference and creativity – not got any of that then? We are natural connectors and relationship builders, our emotions can be used to our advantage as the majority of purchases are made by women. Show me a working mum and I will show you a formidable negotiator, top organiser and budgetary control genius! Business is no longer a ruthless standoff or an all-out battle to kill the competition; these are outdated, male models that worked when there was no other option and I am thankful they did, but today there is a new energy, a more female-centric energy focused on collaboration, values, team harmony, customer inclusion and flexibility. It is our time ladies, we are on!

WE HAVE AN UNREASONABLE FEAR OF FAILURE. I say unreasonable because a fear of failure is a solid motivator for success; however, I see the most amazing, gifted and bright women staying small and insignificant for fear of failure and it breaks my heart. Failure is not personal, it is just the market telling you to move on, the world has changed etc. Markets and customers change all the time. What was in last week is old hat tomorrow and as entrepreneurs we need to keep abreast of this all the time. If we stop looking we will get caught out and this is when failure shows up. Quite often it is out of our control, a new competitor arrives, new technology changes the market overnight etc. What I know for sure is I have learned all my lessons on my knees in sight of failure. It is how I have built personal resilience, honed my passion and raised my game. I, like millions of entrepreneurs, am as proud of my failures as any of my successes and if you really want to walk the exciting and unpredictable path of entrepreneurship you really have to embrace failure as a key element of the journey.

LESSON THREE

I know for sure niche and branding are the double act you ignore at your peril

Branding Clarity or Confusion – It's a Fine Line

Having spent 12 years in the corporate sector as a marketing professional and a further 20 years running businesses I feel comfortable putting my neck on the block and saying I am a marketing expert and I get it. But I am simply amazed at how many people seriously don't! For me marketing is without question the most fundamental requirement for any business. It is the art of getting and keeping customers, profitably. This is surely the premise of any business. No customers, no business! No profit, no business!

For me the biggest and most costly marketing mistakes I see over and over again are related to niche and branding.

Niche – Success is what you say NO to

I am sure we have all experienced the classic networking scenario when you tentatively enquire about each other's business: 'So what do you do then?' Too often the response is confusing, all-encompassing and lacks credibility. For example: 'Well, we develop websites, we also do design and branding, promotional incentives, advertising, room dressing, wedding planning, photography and if you are looking to reduce your phone bills we can do that too.' Ermm? 'So how many people do you employ?' 'Oh just me!'

It is imperative as a new or small business that you define your niche. What can you be number one at? What is your unique specialism? Where do you deliver this in terms of geography? And for whom? All markets are fiercely competitive these days and your skill in defining this will position you clearly and make it easier for customers to make a buying decision and refer you to others.

Here's another example I see all the time: 'I am a life coach.' 'Interesting, so who do you work with?' Response: 'Anyone, anywhere on any issue – relationships, career, business, identity, weight issues, phobias, addictions… blah blah.' How does this response make you feel? Confident in their ability or a little uncomfortable? If they could clearly identify their niche in terms of typical client profile, location, area of specialism, would you feel better? Would they have more credibility?

I spend some of my time in coach mode. Here is how I define my niche: 'I am the entrepreneur's coach, specialising in working with female entrepreneurs with a big vision who are looking to transform their business and themselves in 12 months. I only work face to face from my offices in Cheshire and I only support eight women a year via a bespoke 12-month coaching programme.' Get the idea?

If your child is seriously ill with a rare blood disease would you rather take her to a generalist or a blood specialist? This is the world we live in, you need to pick a specialism and excel in it.

We are living in an emotion economy. People want to feel good and want to help each other, but if you are trying to be all things to all people and frightened of saying NO to anything this can backfire and be detrimental to your professional credibility. Be brave and set out your stall. As you grow the business you can add more products to your niche, and once you have a brand the world of diversification is a real opportunity which leads me to my second learning.

Branding – Creativity Counts

Most new and small business continually underestimate how important branding is. In a noisy market, quite often it is THE ONLY thing that differentiates you from the crowd. But here's what many new starts do: they put all their time, effort and money into developing the business and then come up with a name in less than five minutes! 'Oh I know, let's take my initials and my husband's, combine it with the name of our cat and see if we can get the Latin equivalent'! What does this mean? How will customers connect with it and how does it position the business?

As you know I lead two organisations – The Well Heeled Divas and Girls Out Loud. Both are aspirational businesses and benefit from strong brand investment and recall. Without doubt our marketing has been instrumental in our growth. Can you even consider the boring alternative JK Associates?

It is worth investing in this area of your business, it helps define the business's personality, values and purpose. It helps customers find you, recommend you and love you.

But it is not simply about getting the name and image right. Your brand needs to behave! It must deliver, it must be consistent, and above all it must be authentic.

I have seen so many businesses that have a great brand and position themselves as market leaders then fail at the point of delivery. I am sure you can name several too.

So, to conclude, the key marketing lessons for entrepreneurs: define your niche, become number one in it, create some momentum then allow yourself to be pulled by the niche into new markets.

And secondly invest in your brand. It will be a friend for life if you do and a far more saleable asset when the time comes or the villa in Tuscany calls (or is that just me!).

There is a tendency for 'non marketing' people to assume all of this happens by magic or luck but remember my definition of luck in Chapter Two may throw some light on the subject at this point.

LESSON FOUR

*I know for sure your key job as a leader is to
know your value to your business*

In the same way that the business cannot be all things to all people, neither can you as the boss!

Being an entrepreneur these days demands vision, tenacity, self-belief and most of all courage. Seth Godin is one of my top business gurus and his latest book *The Icarus Deception* was a revelation for me. He stated that entrepreneurs today are modern day artists, with no rule book, no tried and tested system, very little structure, a plethora of new technologies and very few mass markets. Creation is now about connection, leading a tribe, failing often and having absolute faith in your art. The internet has made it possible to create a new kind of business and the rule book is out of the window. He describes the old world of work as:

Bale that cotton; mow that hay; load that barge; fill in this form; obey these instructions, take this test.

And believes the new world of work looks like this:

Start something; figure it out; connect; make the call; ask; learn; repeat; risk it; open; what's next?

I so get this and feel excited to be an artist at this time in history. This shift is so liberating and opens up so many possibilities for so many, however...

There is no guarantee of getting it right, but unless you jump in how will you ever know? Markets and customers are changing all the time. If at first you get no response to your offer or your art, you just make more, better art. Every successful business I have ever been involved in only survived and prospered because it constantly improved and re-energised the way it did business. The mission and vision remained the same, but the way of attracting business and delivering did not.

You don't make art after you become an artist. You become an artist by ceaselessly making art.

Being the boss of your own destiny today is about making a difference in some way and there are no rules for this. Nine times out of 10 you are entering new territory; it may be useful to look at similar companies and people doing similar stuff, but no one will be doing what you propose and in the way you propose doing it. Research and extensive business planning tend to be out of date before they are written and only useful to the dinosaur bank manager and old-fashioned investors who still operate on the 'old system' paradigm. This also means no one can copy you because YOU are unique and your art is your art. I have spent too long worrying about people copying my concept in the past. When we first launched the Divas I remember becoming a tad paranoid and a little angry that I would see my workshop content repeated on other female coaches' websites and hear my words in someone else's voice. I remember being at a women's conference and one of the speakers, a female accountant, had the cheek to use my DIVAPRENEUR pneumonic as the core of her presentation and she had not even done my workshop! Needless to say she was mortified and somewhat lost her train of thought when she spotted me in the audience – but I ask you!

Today I embrace being an artist and know for sure you can copy my words or my concepts but you will never deliver like me nor add the value I do, so there is no point getting angry but I still do not view blatant plagiarism as flattery.

But before I move on, a note about your personal brand – yes, YOU!

YOUR PERSONAL BRAND WALKS IN THE DOOR FIRST

Branding is not just about business these days, even though in noisy, competitive markets it can be the only differential that matters. It is also about your individual brand and the need for you to shine. In fact, your personal brand makes an impact before you even mention your business or product. So what messages do you project and are they getting you what you want? What is your lasting impression? Do people remember you for the right reasons?

I work with entrepreneurs and organisations helping them get clarity on this fundamental issue all the time and feel strongly about the congruency of messages versus actions.

Do you deliver what you promise? Do you walk the talk? Do you live by the values you profess to embrace? Is your story supporting your brand or confusing it?

First impressions really do count, but this is not simply about the clothes you wear or the way you shake hands. It is about your body language, physiology, voice tonality and pitch, the language you use, the values you defend, your beliefs and how you express them, your behaviour and unique personality and, not to be underestimated, your energy.

All of this is hard to fake. If you try, your duplicity is transparent and your brand is destroyed beyond repair. And believe me I have seen many people attempt to own a personal brand that does not belong to them. The end result is never pretty!

The only approach to defining your personal brand is authenticity. Be real, be credible, be true to you because anything less is self-sabotage and pretending you are something or someone you are not is madness and NOT sustainable.

Think about this when you are designing and creating your logo, your website, a presentation or a sales pitch. Or when you meet a potential client for the first time, or start blogging. You must be you, you must own your voice and your opinions.

You are unique, no one can copy you or blossom doing so. Be confident that you will attract and retain the right clients, suppliers and staff by putting you in the room, not some caricature of the so-called perfect business woman or cloned sales person.

People will not always remember what you say, they rarely remember the detail of what you do, but without exception they will always remember how you made them feel. We live in an emotional economy, people want to feel connected, valued and part of something and you can only give them this if you are willing to share the real you in all your Technicolor splendour! This is the key branding necessary to build a tribe, a business, a profile, a community, a career and a legacy.

WEALTH FOLLOWS FLOW

So how do you define your value? Six years ago I discovered a personality profiling tool developed exclusively for entrepreneurs called Wealth Dynamics developed by a global entrepreneur, Roger Hamilton. In the summer of that year I had yet another 'aha moment' when, due to school break and holidays – not mine, everyone else's – my appointments and time out and about slowed down. This forced me to hang out in my office and catch up on paperwork, writing, creative developing and planning, and while this sounds therapeutic and needed, if I am honest, at many moments I wanted to run away!

Now I know you will be thinking why? This sounds perfect! And for some it is, but for me too much time alone, contemplating and planning without people contact, is a recipe for total meltdown. Try writing a book, Jane!

This is because I understand my flow. Flow is what we do naturally, the stuff we are brilliant at, were born to do and is so ingrained in our personality when we opt NOT to do it we falter or become stressed. So for me, as a star profile, flow is about shining my light outwards to help other people find their passion and their flow; it's about inspiring and supporting others to find their greatness; it's about connecting people and organisations to my brand and creating momentum; it's about selling and promoting and talking. And all of this does not happen with me sitting alone in my office, however hard I focus!

Flow for a star profile is all about brand attraction. Stars use their unique personality to create a brand. It is personal and so is their business model. They shine their high energy and natural charisma outward to create leverage for others. Think Oprah, Anthony Robbins, Barrack Obama and Jamie Oliver.

Sitting behind a computer screen makes Jane a dull Diva!

My creativity is so linked to other people I am likely to come up with my best ideas in conversation, as opposed to looking at a blank sheet of paper or a computer screen. Believe me, writing this book was a major challenge!

Over these past few weeks I know I stepped out of my natural flow because work has felt hard and my innate rhythm has been disturbed. Never was this more apparent to me than after spending a day in flow – speaking at a network, followed by lunch with one of my Girls Out Loud Ambassadors finishing with a meeting with five women in a large corporate looking to engage with my cause. By the time I arrived home I was buzzing and recognised my flow all over again.

It is so important to understand this. If you run a business this is your core value to your business and is how you should spend most of your time. If you work for someone else then again flow is your best contribution to your team and the business's bottom line, but in reality for most of us flow eludes us and we end up a round peg in a square hole.

So why? Most organisations from school onwards encourage us to be compliant and obedient. Being a generalist is prized and a focus on weaknesses takes precedence over our success, so we learn how to survive and excel based on other people's rules and definitions. Organisations are hierarchal and advancement is about delivering to a set of criteria even if this means we need to step outside of our natural flow to do this. By the time we hit our stride in our thirties very few of us are in flow, we have just learned how to get along doing what is asked.

As I now understand my flow, I can recall all the moments in my life where I have been out of sync. At school I excelled at communication subjects – English, history, RE, drama, basically any subject where I could tell a story, engage an audience and stand up in class and perform. But my weakness was always maths so I was singled out for extra tuition, and guess what lessons I was forced to forfeit in order to get this extra maths in? Yes, you guessed, the ones where I was in flow!

When I worked in the corporate sector, again I excelled at people development. I was a natural leader and known for my investment in others, my team was always rocking and my chosen profession meant lots of presentations, winning pitches and brand attraction. My weakness was budgetary control and financial management; I hated numbers and so several times at appraisals it was suggested I had a sideways move to a more financial remit before promotion was a reality. This generally resulted in me leaving the company and getting back in flow somewhere else.

Flow is easy and because it is effortless somehow we do not value it as much but what is easy to one is purgatory to another. Standing up and speaking in front of thousands of people feels natural to me and I shine in the spotlight and think well on my feet; writing a book is hard. To others, public speaking is a top fear and working back of house is flow. We are all different and it is important to know these idiosyncrasies in business more than anywhere else because if it feels too much like hard work you will quit.

Wealth Dynamics (WD) is a matrix outlining eight specific profiles and links flow to wealth. The premise is if you are in flow then you are more likely to attract wealth; learning and earning is a game. When you know the specific game that matches who you are, and then play your game according to its rules, you find your flow. This sounds simple but generally most entrepreneurs have no idea what their natural flow is either, as they have spent so long in the corporate system; learning the behaviours of progression, their natural flow is almost invisible. Recognising your value is fundamental to growth.

Define your value and delegate the rest – one of my top mantras. Now I know this cannot necessarily happen overnight as businesses need to create income to invest in people resources but you can get creative in how you do this by engaging in service exchanges, associate relationships, appointing ambassadors or advocates etc. For example, in the early days of The Well Heeled Divas I needed some input from a strategist with the total opposite flow to me, a lord profile, someone who values numbers over people, is a financial genius, loves looking at spreadsheets and understands all the financial data necessary to build a sustainable business. I could not afford to employ this person but I knew who she was. I did a deal with her, as I also knew she needed my star profile energy in her business to advise her on people issues, brand attraction and marketing. It was a no-brainer.

WD is one of the tools that has helped me truly understand my flow and my value to others. But a word of warning. Be careful not to confuse flow with passion. The two are NOT the same. I am lucky as I operate businesses focussed on my passion – to help women and teenage girls recognise their inner star and step up and shine. My flow is about HOW I do that. An individual could be in flow leading a sales team for an international bank but not necessarily be passionate about banking. Flow is about your natural skills, personality and value. Passion is about purpose. The goal is to get both in harmony at some point in your life. So how is it looking for you? Because believe me, you WILL know when this happens.

I recognised several years into my Diva journey how powerful branding can be when I started to hear women who had been on our programmes define themselves as Divas. I would hear them introducing themselves to each other at networks saying 'Oh, are you one of Jane Kenyon's Divas?' I would meet women at conferences/networks who would say things like 'Oh, you are Jane Kenyon, The Diva, I have wanted to meet you for ages. Do you know Carol Jones? She is a Diva too.' Or 'Hi Jane, have you met Sally Kettering? She talks just like you, she must have done your programme and be a member of Divadom.' This was jaw dropping at the time, but I have come to realise that the combined energy of a community, recognition, the need to belong, a star profile in flow and a sassy brand is the route to brand power and attraction for me. And that, my friends, is leverage!

LESSON FIVE
*I know for sure when you understand leverage
the money will flow*

Leverage is about influence, clout, ascendancy. It is the point at which all your hard work, focus and tenacity starts to pay off. It does not happen overnight and quite often it does not happen first time around. Several of the lessons we have already discussed have to be aligned: your mindset, your value, brand, niche, team, product offer and timing. Leverage is how you take a business from doing OK and providing you with a living to becoming number one in your niche and creating serious brand attraction and wealth.

Roger Hamilton defines wealth as value X leverage so let's consider this for a moment. Value in this equation means niche, the space you hold, where you are number one, the platform you sit on, the place you dominate. Now remember, you cannot be all things to all people and it is worth spending some time defining this niche. If you are starting out it will be small in the beginning but as you dominate this niche the market has a tendency to pull you into others and you grow. For example: Girls Out Loud was launched in Manchester; within a year we were running programmes in many North West towns; now four years on we are about to launch our Big Sister mentoring programme in Liverpool, Leeds and East London. In the beginning we defined our niche as:

Girls Out Loud is a social enterprise on a mission to raise the aspirations of teenage girls in the Greater Manchester area by creating and delivering early intervention programmes in schools from one day to 12 months in duration focused on embedding a more empowering mindset, emotional resilience and self-belief.

Now a couple of things about this definition: it tells you what we do and what we clearly do NOT do. We do not work with boys, we do not work with individual girls out of the school environment and we do not work outside the teenage bracket, and at the time of launch we only had the capacity to work in our local area, but believe me this is a huge geographical spread and, in reality, this was probably too big as a starting place!

Over the years our brand has gathered momentum. Our reputation for delivery is now established via our success stories and results; our referrals grow daily; our cause attracts the attention of the regional and national media; we have thousands of women stepping up to volunteer to work with us and be role models to girls. We now have an appointed Advisory Board and a team of national brand Ambassadors. We have some awesome corporate sponsors supporting our work. We are training coaches to deliver our programmes and taking on staff. Our school enquiries are gathering serious momentum and my personal brand is in flow on social media, in print and on the platform attracting opportunities to speak, write and influence. In four years our brand has become synonymous with the national teen identity crisis our girls now find themselves in. A classic case of right place, right time with the right people, right brand and right solution!

Now, do you remember my earlier pleas about niche – success is about what you say NO to? It is very tempting when you set your stall out with passion and almost immediately customers start asking you if you can also do other things that may relate to your niche but are not strictly part of it. For example: 'Jane, do you work with boys?' 'Jane, can you mentor my daughter, she is at boarding school in Barcelona?' 'Jane, can you come in and run a programme for a mixed class of six-year-olds about confidence?' Arrgh! No, No and NO! I could and I know many people would say yes to all of these but this then dilutes the brand, confuses your offer and takes your focus all over the place. In the short term it may get you some one-off transactions and a bit more money in the bank, in the long term it is business suicide!

As you grow your niche expands. Pretty soon I can redefine our niche to have a national focus but we are not there yet. When we hit saturation (not likely in our game!) or our brand becomes strong enough we may diversify in areas that support our core business, e.g. creating programmes for teen mums or delivering training on sexual exploitation and grooming for teachers. Now this may seem like a contradiction but the key is 'when our brand is strong enough'. By this I mean when we have the resources, i.e. the time, the cash, the people.

Unless of course you have infinite resources, then set up a Virgin brand in year one, I dare ya!

If you cannot define your niche in specific terms including product, target audience, geographical reach and benefits then you do not have a niche. The worst way to present yourself is as a generalist, it comes across as lazy, uncaring, boring, mediocre and unskilled. Try this: I am a photographer versus I am the co-founder of a photography company called Nurtured With Love, we specialise in capturing memories of you and your newborn from pregnancy to the first few weeks. Way to go, Louise Wood and Stacey Natar www.nurturedwithlove.com

So along with your personal value to the business (personal brand, leadership and wealth profile) niche is the value part of the wealth equation now to leverage.

There are only a finite number of ways to scale up any business and this is what Hamilton refers to as leverage. How to take your value and duplicate it, scale it, push it further and higher, create more customers, more income and ultimately more wealth.

According to Hamilton, your ideal leverage strategy should fit your wealth profile to ensure you stay in flow – remember wealth follows flow. In order for this to make sense maybe it is time to outline a little more about WD and the eight entrepreneurial profiles.

Whenever I pose the question 'So what is an entrepreneur then?' top of the list is always a creator/ideas person/opportunist, but you know, some of the richest and most successful entrepreneurs in the world did not create a thing, nor did they come up with an idea or unique product. They simply took advantage of what was already out there, capitalised on someone else's idea, made it better, bigger or slightly different.

We do not all have to possess the maverick, innovative and high-frequency creative brains of Richard Branson or Steve Jobs to be successful in business.

Today there are a plethora of opportunities for anyone to get involved in business, but how do you know if this is the right decision for you? For me the key is all about understanding your flow. Your flow is what you are unconsciously competent at, your natural thinking and action dynamic. For example, are you naturally an ideas person, great at starting projects but not so great at finishing? Would you be best described as an intuitive thinker, with your head in the clouds, focused on the future or are you more grounded, with an eye on the here and now, with a preference for caution and research as opposed to gut reaction and feel?

Do you value numbers and facts over people? Is process and the system more exciting than developing relationships? And how would you feel about being positioned as the brand in the business – the person upfront who personifies the brand values and creates attraction?

Wealth Dynamics, like all psychometric tests, is based on I Ching but unlike all others on the market it is focused on revealing your natural flow and route to wealth as an entrepreneur. Hamilton defines only eight types and by aligning those types to some of the world's most successful business men and women helps us to understand our own personal flow.

This is fundamental in helping us choose the right vehicle to create wealth, as each of the eight profiles has a very different strategy for wealth. Richard Branson gets leverage in his business in a very different way than, say, Simon Cowell or Nigella Lawson but they are all multi-millionaires in love with their business and still juiced by it way beyond the need for it.

Before you consider getting involved with any business opportunity you must understand your flow, your path of least resistance. Flow is who we are, not what we do. Successful entrepreneurs focus on their strengths, unsuccessful ones waste time trying to do it all.

As an introduction, here are the eight types.

In bold is my one/two words that sum up the profile:

1. **The Creator** – Builds innovative products, they are high-energy futurists, fast-paced, impatient mavericks who cannot help creating even when they are broke! Examples: Steve Jobs, Walt Disney, Richard Branson, Bill Gates, Anita Roddick
   NEXT

2. **The Star** – Builds an influential, complex brand based on their unique personality and magnetism. They are the brand and excel at creating attraction and noise. They enjoy the limelight and shine their light outwards on others. They need a purpose and are better magnifying their brand one to many as opposed to one to one. Examples: Oprah, Jamie Oliver, Barack Obama, Anthony Robbins
   SHINE

3. **The Supporter** – Builds high-performance teams, great connector and networker, social dynamic and translates value into action through people. Need to hook up with others as wilt on their own. They make the creators' creations sing! Examples: Steve Ballmer (ex-CEO Microsoft), Jack

Welch (ex-CEO General Electric), Meg Whitman (eBay CEO), Sheryl Sandberg (Facebook CEO)
GLUE

4. **The Deal Maker** – Brings people together, well known in niche, good negotiator, grounded in now and has the ability to commercialise their network. Examples: Donald Trump, Rupert Murdoch (media mogul), Simon Cowell (music mogul)
READY NOW?

5. **The Trader** – Is the exact opposite of the creator, overwhelmed by the big picture, tend to be doers and task driven. Masters of timing, grounded and know a lot about the markets they choose to play in therefore create loyalty. Can trade products, people and processes and can make a business from the market left behind by bored or failed creators! Examples: George Soros, Alan Sugar
SAFE

6. **The Accumulator** – Buying and holding assets, ultra cautious, slow and steady, like the eternal tortoise who wins the race. They are well organised, focus on the long term, need lots of data all the time and are introverted. Not great at making the first move to get in the game but once in stay the course. Examples: Warren Buffet, Paul Allen (co-founder Microsoft)
ORGANISED

7. **The Lord** – Controlling cash flow-producing assets, numbers, cash and data driven, risk averse, about efficiency, tend to excel in businesses with few people, lots of process and raw materials like oil, steel and only ever move into very well-established industries where they can implement KPIs and extract more cash value.

144

Examples: Lakshmi Mital (steel baron), Sergey Brin (Google)
HOW MUCH?

8. **The Mechanic** – Creating a better system from the back of house. Perfectionist, will tinker with it until right, show them something once and they are already looking at ways to improve it. All about creating a business that can work without them. Love automation and process, bit boffin-like, no interest in people, would prefer to take people out of the equation altogether and change the way markets work. Examples: Ray Kroc (McDonalds), Jeff Bezo (Amazon), Mark Zuckerberg (Facebook) Ingvar Kamprad (founder IKEA)
PERFECTIONIST

Consider the situation when a creator profile buys into a franchise. How quickly would he/she be out of flow? If a creator cannot turn their ideas into products they will become frustrated and demotivated very fast. This is probably why most successful creators are the franchisor NOT the franchisee. How about a lord joining a network marketing company? Or someone with a star profile running an internet business where they are invisible? Nobody puts Oprah in the corner!

So as a general rule, if you are a people person, need connection, interaction and external validation to shine you are likely to be a star, supporter or deal maker and your best route to growing a business is related to people. If you have the opposite dynamic and prefer process, numbers, research and detailed operational planning then you are probably a mechanic, lord or accumulator. However, many stars build a business with online products and processes and many mechanics have supporters upfront leading their team and developing their business. No profile can work alone and most business models need input from many profiles; the key is that you know your value and stay in flow.

THE ART OF LEVERAGE

The chart below defines the standard options to scale up a business – i.e. get more customers, deliver more, make more money.

PEOPLE	PROCESSES
Build a team – employ staff, short-term contractors, freelance operatives, exchange service contracts, non-exec board etc.	Develop an ecommerce strategy and automate as much of the delivery process as possible
Engage Stars to endorse your products/sell on your behalf – they are masters of attraction	License your IP, materials, brand and/or technology
Create affiliate sales programmes	Create a franchise model
Create strategic alliances and partnerships	
Recruit brand ambassadors and advocates	
Appoint agents and distributors	

So leverage is about understanding your flow and choosing the right model to scale up your offer. Leverage is the point in a business life cycle where it all starts to look interesting, the tipping point. It is the time for investment and making some of the big strategic decisions and I so wish more women arrived at this point in business as opposed to creating a job with no pension, no holiday pay, no security and no team.

LESSON SIX

*I know for sure finding your passion is the
route to sustainability*

**'Find out what makes ya
heart sing, then do that.'**

Whenever I speak to groups
of women and I ask the question 'So, how many of you
jump out of bed every morning with utter bliss and excitement about the day ahead,
anxious to tune into your passion?' I am always saddened
by how few people raise their
hands.

Why does this elude so many of us? When do we give up
searching? When do we stop dreaming? On average in a group
around 10% will raise their hand in response to having found
their passion. When the group is exclusively entrepreneurs the
percentage rises significantly to around 40% but this still means
thousands, if not millions of people are living a life of mediocrity and simply going through the motions, living for the
weekend or in permanent limbo waiting for something better
to come along. Why?

I think many people think finding their passion has to be this
huge light bulb moment or be completely altruistic to count,
they think one morning they are going to wake up with this
foolproof business plan, and because it is their purpose somehow the way ahead will be revealed like some kind of vision
or divine intervention! Oh if only! Because they think this is
a spiritual process they either do nothing or feel it is not for
them.

Well the bad news is if you're doing nothing, you get nothing so unless you are prepared to enter the race, good luck retiring with a company pension, having spent your prime years working on someone else's dream!

How Do I Find My Passion Then?

In my experience very few people uncover their passion early on in life, but I accept there are those who decide at an early age on their vocation and pursue this with love and energy for all their working life – for example, nurse, inventor, barrister, rocket scientist, entrepreneur, working with animals, volunteering to help the poor in developing countries. This is admirable and these individuals are guided but they are the minority. Most of us bounce around, drifting from one job to another, toe-dipping in careers by accident or because we think we will like them; studying a certain profession because our mates are doing it, or the money looks good; taking any job that pays to support our family; playing second fiddle to the bread-winner and just working part-time anywhere to support the household; sticking at the job with misplaced loyalties hoping promotion will bring new challenges and feeling trapped in the system, and so on. Ring any bells? Most of us can carry on like this for years before we hit a crisis point and think 'is this it?'

This crisis can happen anytime but tends to be more prevalent for women in their mid-thirties and men in their early forties. It is the eternal mid-life crisis but it is kicking in younger and younger. Recently I coached a young woman in her twenties, a newly qualified lawyer who had only been in full-time employment for two years but she knew she had made a mistake. She hated the job, the environment and the firm she worked for. She was disappointed that the job was not what she had been sold at school and university, the paperwork was overwhelming and where she thought she would be helping people she actually spent most of her days battling office politics and filling in forms. She wanted out but had no idea what to do next and felt guilty that the past seven years of study would be redundant. She felt trapped and was becoming more and more stressed and unhappy every day. Her story is not unusual, is it?

I was in my mid-thirties before I started to uncover my purpose. I did not stumble upon it, every step in my journey was leading me there. The one constant in all my life has been my interest in people, but if anyone had told me that from my mid-thirties I would be working exclusively with women and girls I am pretty sure I would have laughed out loud and said no way – all that jam making, crafts and pink is not for me! I love men and feel far more alive in mixed company, but the more women I met through my business ventures the more my intuition started to direct me and I realised I had a gift for switching the light on for others. The fact that these 'others' tended to be women surprised me at first but I now know this was always the intention as my journey is empowering to women and I recognised I had a gift to inspire and motivate women to believe in themselves as I have always believed in me. Today I cannot conceive of doing anything else, my passion is all consuming and hand on heart I love working with women – they are so honest, open, warm, caring, supportive, non-judgemental, real and have a gender-specific ability to get in rapport and connect emotionally, fast. I love this. Every day they teach me, surround me with love and stand alongside me on our onward journey.

I share this with you to show you that uncovering your passion is not always a baptism of fire, it can be revealed to you gradually over years but you must be ready and you must be listening! By ready I mean you must have done the work on you.

Sometimes we all have to get off the roller coaster we call life and do some navel gazing, how can we find our passion if we cannot even find ourselves? If you do not know who you are, what is important to you, or what you are capable of, it is unlikely that your mind will connect the dots and reveal your purpose anytime soon. But this takes courage. How courageous was that 20-something lawyer to admit she hated her job, the well-respected profession she had just spent seven years training to enter? How courageous was it of her to stand up and say this out loud and do the work on herself to start a new journey, to have to deal with all the fallout from walking away from a 'good job', to have to answer the naysayers and all the people who had supported her financially and otherwise to get there in the first place?

Exploring your true purpose is not for the faint hearted or the weak willed. It takes gumption, it means you may fail; it means you may have to walk away from financial security in the short term; it means you may have to change your lifestyle; it means you may have to admit to taking some wrong turns; it means you may have to put yourself first for once. Yikes! Really? Sounds very uncomfortable for us women, eh? The eternal people pleasers, fixers and rescuers!

If you are at this crossroads now, I suggest you start the process by doing some reading, maybe attending some personal development seminars or get yourself a coach, they will ask you questions you may not ask yourself. It is a liberating process, you just need to surrender to it.

However, a word of warning: I see so many people who have become personal development junkies. By this I mean they keep doing all the courses but never do the work on themselves, so although they may be able to quote every guru, regurgitate every mantra and have a pretty empty bank account, they're no closer to finding the pot of gold at the end of the rainbow! I think these people are vulnerable and the industry is not great at identifying them and channelling them; however, I have worked with many of these people and generally their purpose is staring them in the face! They have become so addicted to the process they fail to recognise the obvious. To these people I say stop searching, just be and do!

Now, back to passion and entrepreneurship. Today, business is about making a difference, everything else is simply wallpaper. To stay in the business for the long haul you must be driven by something more than money. The need to make a difference is strong in most entrepreneurs, in fact this may be the reason they stepped up in the first place. Even businesses that make widgets may do this to fund a legacy to provide fresh water wells to people in war-torn, developing countries. The passion is not always up front and personal. Branson is passionate about funding projects to understand climate change; Oprah is passionate about educating girls in Africa; Jamie Oliver is passionate about children learning about nutrition and cooking at an early age. Get the picture?

Often the passion is the business. The Well Heeled Divas and Girls Out Loud are all about my passion to empower and inspire women and girls to recognise what they need to do, to shine. It does what it says on the tin and believe me, when people meet me they know for sure this is what juices me. Passion is contagious, and when it oozes from your business brand and philosophy you are on your way to something sustainable.

Growing any business today demands diligence, so to attempt to do this in a sector or industry you are not that interested in is a sure-fire way to quit when the going gets tough. The only thing that keeps you sticky and gives you the courage to ride the waves is being 100% passionate about what you are doing. Regardless of the industry you are in, nothing is recession proof and the low balls will come. Even when you think you have mastered the rules of the game, the game will change and you will have to change with it or surrender to failure.

Girls Out Loud has been a tough journey and continues to present us with challenges at every turn. As an entrepreneur grounded in a commercial philosophy, entering the third sector alone is challenge enough, but then add to this the complexities of generating funding for a cause where the need is clear but neglected; engaging and working with schools; working around the laborious and often unfathomable child protection and risk assessment procedures and managing a team of over 3,000 volunteers and it's obvious to see the motivation needs to be more than money. This business has been built on sweat capital, passion and absolute commitment and four years down the line I am still not able to draw a salary or employ the team necessary to create serious momentum. We punch way above our weight due to the many women who share our passion and donate their time and skills to our cause. We have a solid brand, an amazing track record and today the demand for our programmes continues to grow, at a time when public and charity funding is in decline. This will not deter us, we will find other ways to fund our work, we will harness the corporate sector, wealthy donors and a team of fund raisers and we will be victorious!

I know for sure without my passion for this business I would have walked away within two years. I could not have imagined the complexities of this market, nor the lack of funding or recognition of the teen crisis we find ourselves in. Our approach to this challenge is all about mindset and empowerment by focusing on improving self-belief, emotional resilience and confidence, and although many decision makers in the education sector recognise the power of this and find the resources to invest in their girls, the budget pressures and the target-driven education environment in which we now find ourselves in the UK restricts investment in areas that are considered extracurricular. The frustrating issue for us is without investment in the latter, educational achievements are a wish at best!

Passion is the only thing keeping me in the game! I am driven by the need to influence the status quo and to change the lives of as many teenage girls as I can. It will be my legacy. In a world where you can be anything you want, why would you choose to live on benefits, become a single teen mum, play it safe and stay small and insignificant, refuse to step up for fear of failing, care more about your 'hot monitor' than your potential and remain an invisible face in the crowd rather than celebrate your uniqueness? I am on a mission, stand back!

I implore you to do the work and find your passion. It will make all the difference and the world deserves your best shot. There is a reason you are here, now, on planet earth – find it!

LESSON SEVEN
I know for sure when you recognise peers matter
you will raise your game

'You become who you hang around with. Keep ya wise birds close.'

I have already waxed lyrical about the importance of peers but when you become an entrepreneur this is even more of a game changer.

Running a business can be a lonely place. It is problematic to share your concerns with your team and even harder to bounce potential ideas around when you are the boss. You need to be seen to be in control, you are the chief motivator and no one wants to see your weaknesses. On the days when it is all going pear shaped and a job at the supermarket checkout appears desirable we all need someone to call to who understands our plight. A fellow risk-taker who gets we are just having a bad day, a blip, a moment of vulnerability. The only people who can be your sounding board in these circumstances are fellow entrepreneurs, individuals who are also putting their life on the line in pursuit of creation, independence and purpose.

The life of an entrepreneur is enriched by having a team of other entrepreneurs on side. The more diverse the better as the characteristics that bind you are bigger than a sector or geography. The only people that understand risk are fellow risk-takers; the only people that understand creation are fellow creators and the only people that understand business success are fellow winners. We are artists and as such are pioneering into new territory every day. I often describe being in business as like the first day in a new job EVERY DAY.

Entrepreneurs are not immune to moments of doubt or days when it just doesn't seem to flow, we all need an outlet for a rant and a little motivation now and again and nurturing a peer group is the way to go. Now I know it sounds easy but where do you find these people? Well once you become proactive in your search you will be amazed. I think sometimes we go about our business blind to those around us and only think people in our industry have something to bring to the table. The world of social media is teeming with groups of like-minded people, you can go to a network meeting every day for breakfast, lunch and dinner and still not get around them all. There are 800 female-only networks in London alone! The internet is teeming with female-only portals, circles and communities and several organisations like The Well Heeled Divas who will do the hard work and develop a peer group for you. I facilitate Diva Powerteams four times a year for groups of 12 entrepreneurial women at a time and I love them. The leverage I have seen happen in the room when 12 like-minded women decide to support each other and share their wisdom, connections and experience is magical. But don't take my word for it, here are some current Powerteamers sharing their views...

"Jane is warm and perceptive, with a great sense of humour. Her passion for helping others find themselves and their core strengths in a businesslike manner is inspiring. Jane helped me to really understand my value and belonging. I have been a member of one of Jane's fabulous Diva Powerteams for nearly a year now and it has helped me to think differently and behave differently for the better, with a greater sense of direction and purpose. More than this though, the group are my friends and supporters."

Sally, Senior Manager at Astra Zeneca

"I have had the pleasure of being part of one of Jane's Diva Powerteams, and what a Powerteam it is! I have had the opportunity to meet some amazing women with an aim to share life experiences, thoughts and business acumen. Being in business can sometimes

be a lonely place, but getting from A to B is now that much easier thanks to Jane. Not only do I feel connected to the women in my Powerteam on a business level but I also feel that I have made some great friends for life, who I can always call upon as and when I need. I would recommend this experience to anyone looking to excel in their professional AND personal life!"

Tasnim, Lawyer in big city practice

And just a word about networking...

To network or not – Is this the question?

As someone who has generated well over £2 million in revenue from networking over the last 10 years the answer to this question is a no-brainer! But, and it's a big BUT – I am a people-centred entrepreneur. I am in my flow on my feet, upfront and out and about. The thought of walking into a room wall to wall with strangers is a serious challenge for many but a room full of possibilities for someone like me!

However, this view is NOT universal. For many the temptation to 'give it a miss this time' is too great to fight against. You see some people are natural 'front of house' and others more comfortable orchestrating behind the scenes, and in my view it is pointless spending time and money cajoling them to reverse their roles. We should empower people to shine and this only happens when we allow them to stay true to their personality.

I love meeting new people and therefore I am a natural networker but it is not simply about building rapport at the event that creates leverage. The clue is in the name – networking. The work carries on long after the initial introduction. Relationships need to be nurtured and kept alive and this requires proactivity and more people skills.

There are a myriad of workshops and seminars on the art of networking, promoting the rules of the game, like:

- How to perfect the correct handshake

- Which side of your lapel to wear your name badge (what if you don't have a lapel?)

- How to introduce yourself

- How to work the room

- How to create your elevator pitch

And if networking is a daunting prospect for you, some of this stuff may help, but if you are a natural they are totally unnecessary and likely to hinder your flow.

At its core networking is about relationship building NOT selling. So often it is seen as either a bit of a jolly or a competition to see how many business cards you can collect and give out.

But the bottom line… in today's referral-driven business environment, networking is the cornerstone of many marketing plans and here to stay, so ignore it at your peril. Just think carefully about who is the best person to send along to represent your business. It might not always be you.

And finally, take it from Branson

I often start my keynote when addressing an audience of entrepreneurs with this question:

'If Richard Branson woke up in your bed tomorrow (not with you in it!) with your life, your bank account, your business and your potential how long do you think it would be before he was a millionaire?'

Answers range from one month to two years but the reality is he would be able to make this happen in the time it takes to make a phone call. He would simply call his pal Bill Gates and say 'Hey Bill, in a bit of predicament here, got a great business with bags of potential but need a cool million to take it to the next level fast. Can you wire me the funds ASAP?'

You see, Branson recognises the importance of a sound network. Do you?

To conclude...

Be bold, be brave and believe in your idea, champion your art, build your tribe and leap! You will learn all you need to know on the journey.

PART FOUR

SSSh! THE THREE SECRETS – SUPERWOMAN, SISTERHOOD AND SEXISM

'Embrace sisterhood. Without it we are stepping back 100 years and starting again.'

CHAPTER ONE
HAVING IT ALL – SERIOUSLY?

*The day you let go of the need to be perfect
is the day you discover who you really are.*

I spend a considerable amount of time sitting in coffee bars waiting for meetings, or killing time in between meetings etc. and as a serious people watcher I am exhausted watching and listening to (can't help it – all in the name of research!) professional women multi-task, multi-think and multi-process on high speed every precious second of their down time. The men are generally relaxed, having a social chat, a giggle, discussing football scores, their career plans or what they are doing at the weekend, while the women are talking at 90 miles an hour, stressing about never ending 'to do' lists and life choices. The most popular topics on the table tend to be: organising childcare and child activities; personal grooming; holiday organising; the male idiot on the fourth floor making sexist comments again; what to wear to a charity event a week next Thursday; what books should we be reading; is it acceptable to wear red shoes with navy suit; are we eating enough superfoods; should I have Botox; who is on the latest fad diet and does it work; can you believe I put the washing out this morning and now it is forecast rain, and so on...

Honestly, how do we do it? Why do we do it? Personally I think we are reeling from this notion of 'having it all'. Well I don't know about you, but I don't remember asking for **IT** all and I am not entirely sure what **IT** is. If having it all means having to plan your life with military precision to keep all the plates in the air, or wearing so many badges you are moments away from a full-on identity crisis on a daily basis, or wrapping your superwoman cape around you like a straightjacket, then you can stick **IT ALL** where the sun don't shine!

I feel like we are being punished for even suggesting we are as capable as men in the workplace or even thinking that equality could work. Whenever I hear the words 'having it all' I feel like I am getting a dressing down from some old Dickensian headmaster: 'See dear, you wanted it all and now you have it. Not all it's cracked up to be is it dear? Well now, what are you going to do? May I suggest you get back in the kitchen with renewed vigour and all will be forgiven?'!

But I have to object. We do NOT have equality, it is an illusion, one that a certain genre of men love to throw at us like a weapon with their 'told you so' accusations. But they are wrong. The playing field is absolutely NOT level: we have no political power, only one in five MPs are female; we have no economic parity as the pay gap continues to widen; we occupy too few places at the top of the corporate tree, only 17% of senior jobs are held by women; and we certainly do not have freedom from violence with domestic abuse on the increase and the conviction rate in rape cases standing at a mere 6%, with up to 95% of rapes not even reported. Men and women are categorically NOT equal in society and this cannot be ignored any longer.

WHAT DO WE WANT? WHEN DO WE WANT IT?

Personally, I believe this race for it all has diverted us from the task at hand, or maybe it is all part of the same challenge? To be accepted into the world of work and business as women, to be paid the same as men for the same job, to progress without having to take on male characteristics (if this is not our authentic position), to be offered a seat around the top table if we have worked for it and want it, to have access to affordable childcare and flexible working hours, to be respected by our male colleagues and put an end to sexism, to have the same pension as men, to reposition maternity leave as family leave and see men taking a more active role in parenting, to feel safe walking down the street, to increase the number of women in public life so girls see powerful, female role models across the board and feel certain this is normal. I could go on but you get the message?

I accept we have made huge leaps in all these areas but I am an impatient woman and in many areas the pace has slowed down so much we are in reverse and I find the sexual exploitation of women in the media, sexism in the workplace, violence in the streets and our own home and growing misogyny unacceptable.

Throughout this chapter I intend to share some scary facts on where we are. I hope these help you get to the place many of us are at. The tipping point is different for each of us as we have all had different experiences. However, I do not have to have been raped to campaign for more support for victims and a more effective legal process to encourage women to press charges and secure convictions; I do not need to have experienced sexism in business to know it exists and want it banished, nor do I need to have given birth to empathise with the plight of working mums. Pretending all of this is not happening or is over exaggerated, or accepting it is all part of the rich tapestry of life, or worse still, blaming the victims is not going to get us where we belong. I just hope sisterhood prevails and we all unite to get this show back on the road soon – well no, not soon. NOW!

SCARY FACTS – UK based

- On average more than two women a week are killed in the UK by their partner or former partner. Coleman & Osborne 2010

- A woman is raped in the UK every six minutes.

- Only 15% of female victims of serious sexual offences reported it to the police. Ministry of Justice, Home Office & Office of National Statistics 2013

- Women hold less than a quarter of the seats in parliament and only four out of 23 cabinet positions are held by women. www.gov.uk

- At the current rate it will be more than 150 years before an equal number of women and men are elected to English local councils. The Centre for Women and Democracy 2011

- One in three girls aged 16-18 have experienced unwanted sexual touching at school. YouGov 2010

- One in two boys and one in three girls think it is sometimes OK to hit a woman or force her to have sex. Zero Tolerance 1998

- Nearly 70% of female university students have experienced verbal or non-verbal harassment in or around campus. NUS, Hidden Marks Survey 2010

- 43% of women in London aged 18-34 have experienced sexual harassment in public in the past year. YouGov 2012

- 84% of front page articles are dominated by male subjects or experts. Women in Journalism study 2012

- Women working full-time in the UK in 2012 earned 14.5% less than men; in the city of London the pay gap rises to 33%; in the finance sector the pay gap rises to 55%. Fawcett Society 2012

- One in eight women have left a job because of sexual harassment. Slater & Gordon 2013

- More than 70% of recruitment agencies have been asked by clients to avoid hiring pregnant women or those of childbearing age. UK Equalities Review 2007

- 94% of all women's magazines have a picture of a model or celebrity on their front cover who would be considered thin, if not clinically underweight. The average model is now thinner than 98% of the female population.

Breathe Jane... let's think a little about how we arrived here...

THE CENTENARY – A CHANCE TO HONOUR OUR SISTERS WHO GOT THIS PARTY STARTED!

I cannot help but be moved by all the Great War centenary cel-ebrations at the moment and being married to one of the UK's leading WW1 historians it is a period in history never to be forgotten in my house. The courage and tenacity showed by our nation has moved me to tears on many occasions over the past few months.

Then I watched Kate Adie's awesome documentary on the role and changing economic power of women during the Great War and I had a serious 'aha moment' about our journey.

I looked on in awe as women from all social classes stepped up to do work seen as the exclusive domain of men pre-war. Wom-en worked down the mines and in the shipyard. They deliv-ered the post, worked the land and kept the war effort going by putting their own lives at risk in the munitions factories. They nurtured the sick and wounded, policed the land, put out fires and joined up but it was made very clear to them at every turn that these jobs were only theirs **'for the duration'** and when the men returned they would have to revert to their previous status. This was my 'aha moment'. I recognised that this was the real start of our battle for equality.

Adie pointed out that men feared the feminisation of work would downskill their jobs when they returned, as women would work for less and were less skilled than men. They also felt women demanded less than men as their needs were cheap-er. Oh how my hubby chortled out loud at that one I can tell ya!

On reflection, I can understand this dilemma perfectly from both sides. The men were away from home fighting the blood-iest war in our history and in need of normality when they returned, yet the women had been released from domestic drudgery and servility and experienced independence, camaraderie and economic autonomy for the first time and wanted to retain some of this when their men returned.

In essence, both sexes were sold down the river on this one! Life was never the same again and I feel, as women, we have been fighting to retain our economic independence and our right to equality in the workforce ever since.

Depressingly, by 1918 once the war was over, one third of adult women were in employment, exactly the same as before the war, and within 12 years women's wages were 50% less than men's for doing the same job.

The message was clear. It is OK to help out on the home front and respond to the Government's call to persuade your men to sign up in war time, but when they return life goes back to normal and you need to get back in the kitchen!

Unfortunately, this was the ultimate Pandora's Box situation. For the first time in history many women were liberated and had a true sense of empowerment, they had tasted freedom and now wanted a role outside the home, a public life. They wanted to be part of the workforce. They saw themselves differently. Unfortunately, the men were away when this shift happened and so did not get to share it, or prepare for it, or understand it. For them listening to their women talk about a life outside the home was one step too far, treading on their identity and significance at a time when they felt they had already lost enough.

I get this and I do have some sympathy for the men returning from war to a changed country, where their wives wanted more and their daughters more still! It feels as though women changed in a way that men neither wanted nor approved of and we have been banging on the door of equality ever since.

I honour all those women who stepped up and gave the generations after them permission to demand more, to be heard, to play their part in the economy and public life and to find true fulfilment. I wonder if they are looking down on us today and smiling. Was the plan that we could go out to work but only if we did not expect men to change? Is it OK to bring in an income so long as we never forget that childcare and domestic duties are our sole responsibility? If we want more we can have more so long as we do not expect our men to change or accommodate our need for more. Interesting dilemma, eh?

Now before you turn off, I know there are many awesome men out there, I married one of them. My objective is not to alienate the good men, but I have to call it how I see it. Our emancipation came from necessity. Our country needed us and we stepped up, I think the campaigning going on before and after via the suffrage movement may also have been an indication of our misgivings but the war changed everything for men and women, and clearly we were not and are still not on the same page.

Here is what I see...

CHOICES LEAD TO NEUROSIS

Being a modern woman today is fraught with anxiety and life envy – bold statement, eh? Let me explain.

As women living in the western world the lives we are living are nothing like those of the women that have gone before us – I defy anyone to find serious synergy between their life and their mother's or grandmother's. We are living in a brand new era, for the first time ever we have financial, political, marital and workplace freedom. We can control our reproductive cycle, our bank accounts and our living environment. We are told over and over again we can have it all but in my experience this comes at a cost. The cost is waking up at 3am in a cold sweat worried about whether you made the right decision about work, kids, mother-in-law, husband, boss, dinner choice, shoe selection, previous conversation with a friend, blah blah blah.

This is the neurosis of too much choice! The same conversations are going on over every lunch break all over the western world as women discuss and stress over all these choices and then the envy and guilt starts: has she got it right and I am on the wrong path? Should I be spending more time with my kids? Is working overindulgent? Am I flawed because I am childless? Have I let myself go? Should I spend more time on personal grooming? And so on. I read an article in O magazine recently stating there are only four types of women today:

1. Those who choose work over family and are in conflict about it.

2. Those who choose family over work and are in conflict about it.

3. Those who choose family and work and are in conflict about it – enter superwoman.

4. And mystics – those who have the ability to drown out the constant noise, have found some inner peace and life purpose, recognise their path and follow it with ease.

This really resonated with me. In times past every village had a few mystics, but today to make sense of the noise and the choices it would seem to me we all need to be one! My modern version of a mystic is a Diva!

I think we need to be kinder to ourselves and other women as we are all managing the same barrage of choices on a daily basis, we question everything, all the time, and we allow our inner dialogue to constantly tease us and undermine us regardless of the choices we make.

We may not get everything right but our time here will make it easier for our daughters and the next generation. We must remember we are pioneers, going where women have never gone before. Let's celebrate this and know with certainty that the choices we are making are part of the bigger plan for global female empowerment and are the right ones for us, now.

I genuinely believe we can have it all, whatever ALL means to you, but we need to get real about where our expectations are coming from and adjust our view of unattainable perfectionism accordingly. It is time to face some harsh facts about the equality illusion and get angry about the global treatment of women; this includes waking up to the reality of the negative impact mainstreaming the sex industry is having on our culture and next generation (more on this later). I LOVE being a woman and I feel confident that we will unite in sisterhood to escape from the living doll culture that is professing to be our salvation. Empowerment comes in many guises but, in my opinion, it cannot be found whilst dancing around a pole, half nude, regardless of how this is mis-sold, nor does it wear a cape and a badge saying invincible.

My hope after reading this part of the book is that you dump superwoman and find your inner Diva. She is waiting to come out to play. Her life is more authentic, she is happy to embrace her vulnerability, ask for help from her sisters, say no more often to protect her own liberty and 'me time'. She is guided, sassy, comfortable in her own skin, doing her own thing and an awesome role model to other women and young girls. She does not compromise her values, demands equality and embraces sisterhood.

CHAPTER TWO
SUPERWOMAN – HER SELL BY DATE IS UP!

'Controlling everything does not give you power.
It gives you a blinding headache!'

STRONG WOMAN SYNDROME –
THE STICKABILITY OF SUPERWOMAN

It's Time To Let Go of Superwoman – she who is all controlling, she who will never display vulnerability, she who will never ask for help, she who will never say no. She is feeding our insecurities, she is damaging our self-belief, she is sabotaging our businesses and relationships and she is NOT a great life model to pass on to our young girls. It is time to let her go...

The shoulder pads may be dated but superwoman as an identity and way of being is still alive and well. She is a by-product, a coping mechanism for the 'have it all' culture I mentioned earlier. Over the past 10 years my work with women has given me an insight into the way we are managing our new roles as working women and entrepreneurs, with some interesting observations. In 2007 I coined the term *Strong Woman Syndrome*™. This is superwoman version 2 and goes like this:

STRONG WOMAN SYNDROME© – THE BEHAVIOUR MODEL

Women displaying the behaviour traits of this model are perfectionists. They have high expectations of themselves – they have to be the best mother, best boss, best team player, best social host, best lover, best daughter, best neighbour, best sister, best domestic goddess, best wife, best mum at the school gate, best friend and so on. They also subscribe to the media's definition of Barbie doll beauty, so alongside being the best, they have to do it in heels looking like they have just stepped out of a L'Oreal ad!

As we all know, this self-imposed perfectionism is totally impossible to sustain, so when they fail to deliver, or fall off this self-built pedestal for even a minute, these women are the first to beat themselves up. Regardless of all the amazing feats they may have achieved in the day, the slightest error is the only thing they will focus on and self-flagellations begin for something as tiny as being five minutes late to pick up child from school, burning the tea, forgetting to Sky-plus husband's favourite show.

Because they have such high expectations of themselves and high standards, they believe the people around them have pretty low expectations because no one can do anything as well as them. (Why would they want to?) They will say things like 'you just cannot get the staff, by the time I have shown you how to do this I could have done it myself' or 'no-one else can do this like me.'

Women displaying this behaviour are constantly praying to the 'work/life balance goddess' (at the time of writing, she was still nowhere to be found!) as they take on more and more and slowly turn into scary, dominating control freaks. They end up controlling the whole show at home and work. It's their way or no way.

Juggling can only ever be a temporary state so it's not long before a plate or two come crashing to the floor and things go wrong. But guess what? When this happens strong women simply blame everyone else! It cannot possibly be their fault, remember they are doing everything! Remember, if you blame everyone else for your life decisions and choices you become a disempowered victim. Interestingly, this is a position of weakness not strength. So all the time we think we are projecting a strong, in control woman, underneath we are weak and vulnerable. The two states we fear most.

This is a very confusing model of behaviour. We switch from superwoman to victim continuously, sometimes several times a day or even in the duration of a conversation and we wonder why we are misunderstood. One minute we are in total control, invincible and strutting along in our high heels, the next minute we are a bumbling wreck of insecurities, blaming the world for our plight, feeling unloved, unappreciated and exhausted!

"My career change was quite subtle from employee to management and due to this subtleness I didn't realise for many years that I was striving for perfection in most of my roles – wife, mother, daughter, boss, business partner and client manager. However, life catches up with you and I think as time goes by and, dare I say, you get a little older, you cannot keep up with the pace. It isn't necessarily about the hours you spend rather than the pace of life. All aspects are important and you try to be superhuman trying to juggle all and forget about you as an individual. Guilt is a major player that women seem to hold and this is sometimes the driving force – if I spend time at work, I then need to work

extra hard at home and vice versa. The snowball starts and then you need someone to point out what's going on. This often needs to be someone away from your immediate pressure otherwise you are not likely to take any notice. If you invest in you and talk to someone else about this (I worked with Jane as my coach) in due course you start to realise what you are doing and although a scary feeling, you then find out that the way you have handled things is not always best for you and those around you. Awareness is power."

Jackie, Company Director, wife and mother of two children, one with Asperger's syndrome

CAN YOU WASH UP PLEASE LOVE?

Here is an example of a scenario played out in thousands of households every night...

You and your partner/husband have both arrived home after a day at work. You make the dinner and ask him to wash up. He dutifully embraces the task and after a reasonable amount of time has elapsed you arrive in the kitchen for your inspection.

At this point you call him back to the scene of the crime and say 'I thought I asked you to wash up.' He looks perplexed and replies 'Well I have.' Now you take a deep breath, stand tall and produce your evidence. 'Oh you have? Really? Well you have not swept the floor, emptied the bin, wiped down the worktops or used the special cloth to get rid of all the smears on our stainless steel appliances. You have loaded the dishwasher incorrectly and the casserole dish is still on the hob. And in all the time we have lived together when have you ever seen me put crystal glasses in the dishwasher?'

He/she generally only has two standard replies to this outburst:

1. Well, you never asked me to do all of that, you just asked me to wash up and I did.

173

2. Well, you know what to do next time then, do it yourself.

Thing is, our reply to this rebuff is generally along the lines of 'Right, well I'll do it myself then, like I do everything else around here anyway. Pathetic, if you want a job doing right in this house, you have to do it yourself, blah blah blah!'

Ring any bells? This is an example of strong woman syndrome in action. We demand everything be done to our standards, we control the show, we, in effect, disempower everyone else, then get upset when it goes wrong or does not meet our exacting standards.

Now, before you start screaming at me and fling the book across the room let's talk some more about this.

I know most men are useless in the kitchen or with many domestic tasks. A very good friend of mine coined the term 'domestic dyslexia' in relation to men and I love this! I also know most men want to do whatever is necessary to make us happy. It is just that the two do not always coincide. Incidentally, I am pretty useless at looking after my car, the garden, any equipment/machinery, making fires, fixing stuff and heavy lifting. My husband does all of this unprompted and without complaint and he never asks me to participate or learn any of it! Maybe we should recognise each other's strengths rather than demand we become interchangeable. Just a thought.

It is almost impossible to change other people, particularly men. We can only change ourselves. But magical things happen when we change. Our shift creates a tidal wave around us and is a catalyst for different behaviour in others too.

We all display some strong woman tendencies and this is manageable and part of our charm, but if you control everything in your house and beyond – the budget, the cleaning regime, where you eat, shop, holiday; who does what, when, how and where; you choose your friends, regulate conversations, choose your husband's clothes, what he can and cannot eat – in effect you control the whole show, be warned, this is a recipe for relationship conflict, emotional pain and not an ideal life model to pass on.

How about this comment from a male coaching client of mine, convinced he was having a mid-life crisis and suffering with seriously low self-esteem:

'I am not allowed to eat pies and no point trying to sneak one in 'cos my wife always smells my clothes for evidence when I get home and not worth the nagging followed by the silent treatment if I disobey her.'

A DISEMPOWERED MAN IS AN UNHAPPY MAN

Although I recognise and understand you may feel you have been driven here and have no choice, there is always a choice. If you are controlling you are disempowering your partner and a disempowered man is not a happy man. He generally has two choices in response to being totally controlled:

- He can accept this and sit back and let you get on with it, accepting with apathy your nagging and inevitable outbursts. But this seriously affects his spirit, confidence and self-esteem.

- Or he can step up and attempt to gain back some control, but unfortunately this will not be in the areas you want. He will not be fighting with you as to who cleans the kitchen, negotiates with the nanny or does the weekly food shop.

We have confused control with power.

The strong woman syndrome appears to be a position of strength, but in reality it is a place of weakness. Controlling everything does not give you power, it gives you a blinding migraine! It is emotionally exhausting to think that the only way to demand respect, or to be loved, or to be needed is to DO everything, for everyone, perfectly, all the time.

Real power comes from our authenticity, real people make mistakes, real people learn and grow, real people embrace their vulnerability or what Brene Brown calls their shame. Our shame is the fear of disconnection – if people find out about my weaknesses I will be alone. We are not supposed to be perfect. Superwoman is not strong; she is in fact weakness personified and must go!

THROWING AWAY THE CAPE AND THE INVINCIBLE BADGE

There is a better place to live. A more nourishing place where you are allowed to embrace your vulnerability. A place where you can be true to yourself and be loved for who you are, not what you do or what you look like. A place where being female is a joy, where you can tap into your intuition, passion, emotions and courage. A place where it is OK to ask for help, to say no and to hand over control, sometimes!

"I realised after eight years of running my own business and raising two children that my striving for perfection in all areas was having a really negative impact on my health, my sanity and my relationships. I finally decided to bite the bullet and get a cleaner to take care of the house and even asked my mum for her help when it came to the ironing! I actually managed to ask my husband for help, which he gives willingly, and despite the fact that it goes against my nature, I have a much happier household and a more balanced life – being superwoman isn't all it's cracked up to be!"
Claire, married mother of two running a PR company

Now did I just mention the V Word – VULNERABLITY?

I have coached hundreds of women out of this destructive behaviour pattern and the one belief that is common and the key to hanging on to this identity is the fear of the V word

– VULNERABILITY. Most superwomen see vulnerability as a weakness and fight against it at all costs. This is why they find it hard to let go, embrace failure, accept help or harness their authenticity because their real self feels substandard, not enough, defective in some way. Superwoman has subscribed to the media's view of 'having it all' and these women believe they have to be and look perfect at all times.

I know many people agree with me when I say vulnerability is power because it comes from truth. Real power is about authenticity, making mistakes and learning and growing, living by your own values, embracing failure, having fun, letting go and accepting help once in a while. Showing your vulnerability allows others to step up and take some responsibility, it lets them show you they love, respect and care about you – and who doesn't deserve to have princess days now and again?!

I know this is a complex area and deserves more attention. Whenever I see women struggling to grasp vulnerability, I share my take on it in my relationship where it tends to get magnified. Anyone who meets me will confirm I am a strong woman, known for my resilience and gumption; however, I have my moments and have no issue sharing my vulnerability with my husband, Tony. He knows me better than anyone, because I let him. He knows when I am nervous, anxious, struggling with self-doubt or out and out terrified! I made a conscious decision to give him my vulnerability as a gift when we fell in love. He knows this, feels honoured to accept my gift and treats it with the utmost respect. A win/win.

NEW RULES:

- Dump Little Miss Perfect, embrace the real you. Authenticity is real power, know who you are, your hot buttons, your passion and compromise them at your peril.

- Know that striving for perfection at work and home is fake and weak. The business plan is never done, the website can always be improved, the kitchen could always be cleaner. New mantra: 'Get going and get better'!

- Embrace failure. We are supposed to make mistakes, it builds emotional resilience and teaches us about life. If you are not making mistakes you are not living your best life.

- Accept and give help. This is the new sisterhood. We are not supposed to be completely self-sufficient, we need community.

- Be proud to be an emotional creature, it is not a crime, it is real, get over it!

- Value your uniqueness and teach your daughter to do the same – we are not all supposed to look or behave in the same way.

- Be kinder to yourself. Stop beating yourself up about your life choices and know that your best is good enough.

- And the big one – embrace your vulnerability. Have the courage and compassion to share your story, flaws an' all. If you numb vulnerability you also numb joy.

Strong woman syndrome is discussed in more detail in my first book *Superwoman Her Sell By Date Has Expired. Time To Show Little Miss Perfect The Door!* If any of this resonates with you invest a little more time understanding the behaviour patterns and what you need to do to dump it once and for all. See the resources section at the back of this book.

CHAPTER THREE
BE DEFINED BY WHO YOU ARE
NOT WHAT YOU LOOK LIKE

'Your daughter will not always remember what you say, but believe me she is watching and it is what you DO now that matters.'

Argh! This is a plea from the heart. As someone who spends hours talking to young girls, trying to convince them that they are beautiful just the way they are when they have just spent 20 minutes explaining to me in minute detail everything about their bodies they hate including kneecaps, toes, hairline, fingernails, ear lobes (I kid you not!) feet, thighs, boobs, eyebrows, tummy, back, lips, nose, eyelashes and bums. I am exhausted by our fixation on appearance over experience fuelled by the media but accepted by us and internalised as 'the way it is' the world over. There is always a new trend to make sure we never get ahead of ourselves, triple zero, canckles, thigh gap, designer vaginas and I am so angry that we are infecting girls as young as five with this nonsense – are you?

OUR TEENAGE GIRLS NEED ROLE MODELS MORE THAN EVER – HERE'S WHY

Alongside the conversations with young girls I also hear the other side from women, their concerns surrounding their teenage daughters/nieces/sisters etc. We seem to be bemused by our girls' obsession with appearance over substance; their apparent addiction to social media and why they all want to look the same – like some pumped-up porn Barbie!

Well I thought it was time I put some data to all of this so here are some more of those scary stats and the latest research relating to teenage girls. Take a deep breath...

1. 47% of teenage girls feel the pressure to look attractive is a disadvantage to being a girl. This figure rises to 76% for 15/16-year-olds. This affects self-esteem, alienates girls who dare to be different and has a huge impact on aspirations. Girlguiding UK 2009

2. By the age of 12 over 50% of all girls in the classroom will be monitoring their food intake in some way. Many will be actually dieting, starving themselves or using other stimulants to fight off hunger. UK All-Party Parliamentary Group on Body Image (APPG) 2012 & Girlguiding UK 2009

3. 87% of teenage girls are now unhappy about their body shape. Bliss Magazine Survey 2004

4. One in four teenage girls will self-harm in some way before they leave school. This is often a symptom of point 1 but can also be family stress, exam anxiety or boyfriend issues. World Health Organisation report on Health Behaviour of School-Aged Children 2014

5. 5% of girls aged 12-17 are now prescribed antidepressants. European study carried out by Australian & New Zealand Psychiatry 2014

6. There has been a 12% rise in under-16-year-olds with drink-related problems. Six children a day will be admitted to hospital with drink-related issues. Binge drinking is more prevalent among girls and 25% of girls aged 15/16 admit to binge drinking at least once a week. NHS report 2012

7. Boys as young at 11 are now addicted to internet porn. This has a negative effect on girls as expectations on how to look and what constitutes normal sex are warped. Psychologies magazine 2010

8. Girls are now three times more likely than boys to suffer with depression and anxiety attacks. European Study carried out by Australian & New Zealand Psychiatry 2014

9. Grooming and sexual exploitation is now commonplace in most towns and girls are now initiated and forced to be active in recruiting. Girls and Gangs, a report by Centre for Social Justice 2014

10. The issues around early sexualisation and the internet just keep getting worse. The latest trend, sexting, involves girls sending nude/semi-nude pictures of themselves to boys then the boys forwarding on. Girls are under a lot of pressure to do this as it is now perceived as normal behaviour. NSPCC report on Sexting December 2013

My work with Girls Out Loud takes me into schools every week and here is what I see in every classroom of girls, and I mean EVERY CLASSROOM, the location or the status of the school is irrelevant:

Low confidence, low self-esteem and low aspirations.

Girls getting validation from the way they look, not who they are or what they are capable of.

Confused identity as girls struggle to process overtly sexual imagery, airbrushed celebrities and widespread porn.

Girls choosing safe career options (nursery nurse, teacher) or none at all, due to lack of positive role models. You don't know what you don't know!

181

Low self-respect as poor cues on what is and is not acceptable sexual behaviour, compounded by poor sex education, the media onslaught, reality TV and the internet.

Girls becoming more predatory and aggressive. This is misplaced confidence, copying pop videos, dressing like hookers and generally attracting attention they are not sure what to do with.

SO WHAT DO WE DO?

In my opinion the first thing we all need to do is take some responsibility for the current situation. It is all too easy to step back and blame a diverse range of external factors for why our girls are lost. We need to take the lead, show them the way, be their role models. So how are we doing?

Here's some food for thought:

1. The UK now spends over £2 billion a year on cosmetic surgery procedures. Well over 90% of customers are female. The industry is growing fast and expected to hit £3.6 billion by 2015. Department of Health

2. Three quarters of British women are unhappy with their body shape. Marks &Spencer Survey 2012

3. In the same Marks & Spencer survey six out of 10 women said their body image made them depressed.

4. For UK brides, looking good on their wedding day has become an obsession. British brides now spend more money on cosmetic procedures for the day than they do on their wedding dress! Survey carried out by wedding site www.confetti.co.uk July 2012

5. Pole dancing is now available as an acceptable workout in most UK towns and thousands of women are flocking to the classes.

Need I say more? Young girls will copy what we do, **not** what we say. When we start valuing our natural beauty, falling in love with ourselves and behaving in an authentic way, so will they. Our position as role models has never been more important. So how are you showing up? Let's see...

YOU ARE SO MUCH MORE THAN WHAT YOU EAT – HONEST!

When will we give up our obsession with weight/dieting and the never-ending pursuit of a size 10? It seems that every time I am in the company of women, be it at a professional network or social group, the main topic of conversation is sharing diet regimes, detox plans and weight goals – and to be honest, it is BORING!

Seriously, it is time to change the record. My relationship with food and my body is pretty boring and totally predictable and I know for sure my small talk and conversation is all the better for excluding it! I know the script, I get the self-sabotage, I've got the T-shirt, mug, key fob and every book on the subject, so please, please talk to me about something else.

Tell me who you are and what makes your heart sing. Share with me your greatest challenge and your greatest joy. Inspire me with your story, your passion, your legacy.

We are so much more than what we look like or what we weigh and until we get this don't expect our teenagers to walk free of eating disorders, self-harming or low self-esteem any time soon. If we are overflowing with body hatred and a lack of self-love why do we assume they will be any different?

WHY IS THE SURPRISED BARBIE DOLL LOOK SO APPEALING?

And now to Botox and the never-ending pursuit of youth. I was doing my usual flicking through the glossies recently as I enjoyed my cappuccino and could not help but feel sad at the latest bunch of celebrity women who have disfigured their pretty features with Botox and fillers. I assume the concept of these injections is to enhance your features and stop the ageing process but it very rarely turns out that way, does it? It just makes them look so obviously fake and in most cases distorts their features so much they look like clowns or caricatures of who they are supposed to be. I don't get it. Surely the point of these procedures is discretion and subtlety? And who needs anti-ageing procedures when you have not even hit 30? Yes Jessie J, I am talking to you!

As women the pressure to conform starts at eight years old and continues for most of our life, doesn't it? Why else would some of the world's most beautiful women do this to themselves? Cameron Diaz, Goldie Hawn and even Nicole Kidman – an actress who was known for her porcelain skin and natural beauty. She is now so pumped up with Botox and the rest, her acting career is in jeopardy as she cannot use her facial muscles to express emotion anymore! We are supposed to age, we are supposed to get wrinkles, our skin is supposed to change in texture and appearance. We are not supposed to look like a surprised Barbie doll. I despair! But am I being too hard on these women? Is the pressure to stay youthful so intense they are pushed more and more to experiment with this stuff? Do they see what I see when they look in the mirror? Who is making the rules here? It is interesting when you listen to some men comment on the appearance of some high-profile women that have NOT had any of these procedures done and are more than happy in their own skin, literally! They say things like 'She is looking a bit haggard' or 'She is not ageing well is she?' You see we are so used to the cloned Botox look that when we see a real woman in all her beauty we do not recognise it anymore and this is seriously worrying, I feel. I for one will be celebrating real beauty and real women for the rest of my days, how about you?

DESIGNER VAGINAS – WHATEVER NEXT?

Oh, and now as my blood is on the point of boiling, the fastest growing elective cosmetic surgery procedure in Harley Street at the moment is LABIAPLASTY. Forgive me, but this makes me hyperventilate with rage. What? Why? And most importantly, for whom?

How many more ways can we find to beat ourselves up? What now, our vaginas are not perfect? Who says? Who is defining what normal is? And who says we all have to look like a porn star or a Barbie doll anyway? My vagina is angry about this, so much so that over the past few weeks I have conducted my very own survey. I have asked every man I happen to have been in conversation with (and have a modicum of rapport with, obviously) his views on designer vaginas. Not surprisingly, all of them responded the same. They are bemused, embarrassed, exasperated and sad that we would even consider this.

What world do these women live in? Do they seriously believe that men care or even notice the shape or thickness of their most intimate flower? It is utter nonsense to even consider subscribing to the notion of the perfect vagina and it breaks my heart to contemplate the messages this barbaric, self-hating procedure sends out to our teenage girls.

I feel confident that this is yet another gift handed down to us from the $97 billion sex industry – yes I did say $97 BILLION, this industry is worth more than the combined revenues of Microsoft, Google, Amazon, Yahoo, eBay, Apple and Netflix. When you get your head around this you start to understand some of the issues we are now facing as a society, particularly in relation to the empowerment of women and young girls. Indeed, porn is where most of our young girls learn about their sexuality. It would appear the living doll look is here to stay.

At the moment labiaplasty is too expensive for all, so it remains the surgery of choice for porn stars, strippers and the self-obsessed rich wives club, but how long before having a designer vagina is as easy and acceptable as getting a boob job? A topic of conversation going on in most classrooms among girls as young as 14 years old.

Are you ranting yet? Are you sad? Or are you happy to stay in denial? If we continue to buy into this hype our world is not going to change anytime soon. How about this for a conversation I overheard in my local wine bar some time ago.

It is a few weeks before Christmas and a group of perfectly groomed, cosmetically enhanced women in their late thirties (they could be younger, so hard to tell with so much Botox and filler in their faces and 'cartoonesque' fake boobs!) are all chatting intensely as they move their salads around their plates, God forbid any of them would actually eat it! They are sharing schedules and are very animated about how much they have to do in the run-up to Christmas and the annual family skiing trip in January. Let's be clear, these women do not work, they have wealthy husbands, nannies and household staff, their job is focused on appearance and maintaining the family harmony. The list of activities stressing them out includes hair appointment, tanning, waxing, Botox, nails, then sorting outfits and packing. On top of this they had to confirm outfits for several corporate functions with their husbands over the festive period and try to fit in a few school activities (last on the list, I can assure you). At this point the conversation, temporarily, switches to children and at least four of the women discuss their disgust at the very expensive school all their daughters attend, as a couple of the girls, now 14, had come home asking for boob jobs! They were outraged by this and agreeing on the best response to the Head Mistress as they were all paying substantial school fees and expected more – seriously? Are you sure? Believe me, it was all I could do to breathe at this point.

We need to start joining the dots and we need to do it fast!

CHAPTER FOUR
LET'S GET REAL ABOUT THE F-WORD

'Empowerment is not to be found
dancing round a pole.'

I was not always a feminist. Well, not a full-blown, orthodox one anyway! Never saw the need. I spent all my teens assuming no one other than me existed and in my twenties was so focused on climbing the ladder and being a success I was blind to the sub-modalities around me and had no idea my success could be marred by my gender. As I never had to deal with the children issue I reckon I had a pretty easy ride, so to speak.

Then when I started working with women I had a serious reality check. I was appalled at the sexism in the workplace, the slow progress in board appointments and all senior management jobs, the media machine, misogynistic behaviour on campus and in the playground, and a whole raft of other stuff, and my conscious began to prickle. I was particularly stressed by the level of violence targeted at women and girls and our invisibility in public life, the very place we need to be to create dissonance and start to campaign in earnest again. However, early on in the Diva journey I was silenced, or should I say I allowed myself to be silenced. Every month my partner and I would host a free two-hour event called a Diva Kickstart in several key cities throughout the UK. The objective of these events was to give women a taster of our programmes and position our brand as a community for women to connect, inspire and support each other. I would lead these events and at some point in the evening I would discuss the need for us to stay focused on the end game and continue pioneering for equality as we were a long way from the finish line and our daughters needed our vigilance. Now, I may have been a tad overzealous in my messages as over a period of six months we received a bit of feedback calling us 'man-haters'. As you can imagine, this freaked me out and I immediately cut this section out of our event agenda. In effect, this reaction silenced me for many years as the very last message I was looking to stick was that one!

When the partnership ended and I became the brand, I invested in an image change and new collateral and through my blogs I found my voice again. I still feel the same way about all the inequalities I talked about back in 2008, only now I am not afraid to speak up about the unacceptable treatment of women, as I see the impact this has on teenage girls and this is unforgiveable. In the five years since I started working with teenagers the sexist environment has intensified, not improved; mainstreaming porn has had a disastrous effect on our youth; the media continues to poison our girls' self-esteem; social media has created even more threats to our liberty; violence in relationships is on the up among 16-18-year-olds and surprise, surprise, even though girls outperform boys academically they are still playing second fiddle to them in the workplace. The fear of reversing all the positive wins as I listen to young girls define their future is why I am now proud to be a feminist and why I do not apologise for presenting the facts and sharing my views, sometimes with a hint of anger and frustration but always with love and hope for a brighter, more equal future. I am delighted to see a new wave of young women picking up the feminist baton and making it cool on campus, on the screen and on social media – big respect to Caitlin Moran, Laura Bates, Jennifer Lawrence, Emma Watson, Lena Dunham, Holly Baxter and Rhiannon Lucy Cosslett to name a few.

I feel we have moved backwards not forwards, yo-yoing away from bra-burning and Germaine Greer towards pole dancing and slut shaming. It seems to me the word feminist is used as a weapon against women by sexist men and female chauvinistic pigs and we must rise above it. The time for pioneering and campaigning is upon us, now is not the time to be reasonable and politically correct. Now is the time to embrace the feminist mantra, step up and act.

A storm is on the way, it is time to stand up and say enough. We deserve more respect and until we demand it our daughters will not know it is a given.

FEMINISM – DUMP THE WORD BUT DO NOT FORESAKE THE MESSAGE!

As a foodie and huge fan of the graceful, feminine and smart Mary Berry I cannot tell you how disappointed and surprised I was at her comments on feminism recently. She said 'I think feminism is a dirty word and I don't want women's rights. I love to have men around and I suppose if you are a feminist you get on and do it yourself, so I am not one.' Arrgh! For an educated woman and one of the few women on TV over 45 her comments made me want to scream! And I did! Do I need to list all the benefits Mary has and takes for granted because of feminism? Do I, do I?

Who said feminism means you don't need a man? Can men not be feminists too? And her comment 'I don't want women's rights' – seriously Mary?

Now is not the time to turn our backs on feminism. Whether you like the word or not, please do not get distracted by a word or an old-fashioned, militant definition. All feminists are not tub-thumping, bra-burning and dungaree-wearing men haters. I, for one, love men, I just don't want to be one, nor do I want to be subservient to one.

It breaks my heart to hear educated, successful women disrespect feminism saying 'It is not for me, or 'I would never be one now' or 'We don't need it anymore.' Really?

Try telling that to the 70 million girls around the world who are crying out for an education.

Or the millions of women around the world sexually assaulted, abused and violated every day.

Or the thousands of girls trafficked into the multi-billion dollar sex industry every month.

Or closer to home...

Talk to any group of teenage girls in any school, in any town and try and keep your jaw from dropping as they enlighten you on their world, which includes sexting, starving, cutting, binge drinking, bullying, body hatred, depression, reality TV, porn, cosmetic surgery and the rest.

Our girls need feminism now more than ever. We need the next generation to know they are valued for their mind not simply how 'hot' they are.

If the word feminism does not work for you then reframe it but don't give up on the message of equality, freedom to choose and empowerment. Not now.

And contrary to the myth that young girls don't get feminism, they do, they just don't understand the word. They want to have the same opportunities as the boys, they want to be taken seriously as opposed to being seen as sex objects, and on two areas that were fundamental wins for feminism – contraception and equal pay – they find it hard to imagine how we lived without them, so the cause did something right, eh?

I urge you to stick with feminism for a while longer. We have unfinished business and until we can walk down the street safe, are valued for more than our looks, are allowed to age gracefully, are recognised as leaders whether we have kids or not and have a more equal say in how we are governed, we cannot and should not take our foot off the pedal.

And personally, I subscribe to Caitlin Moran's definition of feminism: 'If you put your hand down your pants and you can feel a vagina and you care about what happens to it, bingo you are a feminist!'

Do not let the male-dominated media own the feminist debate – Hail Sisterhood!

There seems to be a plethora of articles on and offline at the moment discussing the pros and cons of being a feminist, or more to the point, what the word feminism means and if we still need it, or if you are one how you should behave! 'Are you a feminist?' has become the number one question the media are eager to ask women in the public eye, from Michelle Obama to Cameron Diaz, and then dedicate pages of space to their answers so other women can scrutinise and criticise their definition and/or comments. This is definitely NOT sisterhood.

I have ranted about this many times before and it would seem I need to rant some more! I fail to understand what the big deal is here – if you are a woman (or man, for that matter) and you care about your daughter growing up in an equal society, where she is respected and given the same opportunities as the boys and not vilified for her personal choices, or only regarded for the way she looks, then whether you like the word or not YOU ARE A FEMINIST. So let's move beyond the word and get on with the job at hand.

Clearly another agenda is at play here with the media constantly pitching women against each other, ensuring we appear to have totally opposing views on the same subject – this copy is perfect for making us appear confused, lost, angry, indecisive, or just plain stupid. And we are buying into it. More importantly it makes it look like we do not care about each other, or the philosophy of equality that we are supposed to embrace.

This 'sister baiting' plays into the wrong hands every time and disempowers us. We are off message and it is time we woke up to the real issues feminism is about rather than continually justifying that feminism is not about hating men or burning bras or wearing dungarees or power dressing or being viewed as ball breakers when we reach the top. I am so bored of all this, aren't you?

Furthermore I am also bored of people saying you must be a bad person and an equally bad feminist if you dare to utter one word against another woman. I appreciate after what I have just said this may seem like a contradiction but feminists are human beings, not saints! No one is immune to an opinion and just because you don't like what Beyoncé is wearing does not mean you hate her or disrespect her life choices. We are not made of sugar and spice and all things nice. We are bold and brave, nurturing and collaborative and pioneers of change and every step we take demands courage and conviction. Time to step it up, gals. Walk it, Work it, Be it!

Sister baiting is playing into the wrong hands and we are blind to the impact.

I, like many people, feel disappointed and ashamed at the reaction to Maggie Thatcher's passing from many corners of our community especially the social media fraternity. The level of hatred and juvenile name-calling from both men and women is unnecessary and when women turn on other women like this I am overwhelmed by sadness.

Maggie's political ideology, in fact her party's ideology, and her personal character should not be confused. Whether you agree with her party's administration or not she was this country's first and only female Prime Minister and respected all over the world for her strategic leadership, courage and determination. Is this vile character assassination fair?

At the time of her death I was asked to pen a few words on her legacy for a national business magazine. This is what I wrote:

Maggie's Legacy

That it's possible to be yourself and bag the top job in a male-dominated world. Oh yeah! Love or hate her, Maggie was an alpha female, authentic and true to herself, taking no prisoners and making no apologies for who she was, how she behaved and what she believed.

She gave women permission to raise their game and subconsciously I am sure she inspired a generation of business women.

To say she was not feminine or a feminist is naïve. Her influence on the international stage was a masterclass in feminine power, and her focus on getting the job done versus likeability was a rare but much needed trait in women.

She said what she meant and meant what she said. A quality sadly lacking in today's politicians and in my book any woman that has First before her job title deserves respect.

Furthermore she led this country through tough social, economic and political change and yes she made mistakes; yes her judgement faltered sometimes; yes her ego got the better of her sometimes and yes she became far too dominant in the end, but let's not vilify her for her imperfections.

She was real, certain of her beliefs, willing to make decisions and unwavering in her principles even if this meant her popularity suffered. Is this not what we are all striving for – to be authentic? Just because we may not share her view on authenticity does not mean it is wrong. Being authentic is not fake unless it's your version! It is living your life by your own truth, not that of others, and no one could accuse Maggie of being a people pleaser.

It confuses me to hear women constantly saying how she did nothing to help the advancement of women and she was not a feminist. These comments are so contradictory when I also hear women talking about how much they want to be valued on merit, not simply their gender. This is the argument always put forward to oppose quotas. Did we expect Maggie to only employ other *women? Is this the only way we would accept her as a feminist? For me, the definition of feminism is about embracing equality of opportunity, about my right to choose on a level playing field. Are we saying Maggie did not subscribe to this? Did she not succeed in a meritocracy?*

As women we also recognise we have a complex relationship with success and likeability, in that we often sidestep success if it means it may make us unpopular. We value being liked too highly. Leadership is not a popularity contest and Maggie is the proof of this. Her courage to ride this in order to stay true to her political principles, regardless of whether you agree with them or not, is surely to be admired?

I am starting to sound like her biggest fan now, and interestingly enough this is not true, but I think it is cowardly to hurl abuse at someone's gravestone.

Before you judge her on a personal level, take a look in the mirror. Do you know what you stand for? Are you living a life aligned to your values and beliefs? Do you stay true to your principles even if it means you may be unpopular? Are you certain of your purpose and passion? Are you playing full out and showing the world your real authentic self?

I am pretty sure Maggie would have had a giggle at our expense at some of the jibes directed at her and let's be honest, if the woman is remembered for anything she certainly gets people passionate about politics – can you really say that about ANY of our politicians today?

EQUALITY IS AN ILLUSION UNTIL THE VIOLENCE STOPS

Let's not take our foot off the gas yet, if you don't like the word feminism dump it, find something else you do like – how about Diva? And to finish this section a final word on violence against women, a subject surely none of us can debate or disagree on?

194

It is a global crisis and equality will remain an illusion until it stops.

As part of International Women's Day last year I was asked to take part in a mini film produced by Oxfam called 'Are We Equal?' A camera was put in front of me and I was asked to respond to the question 'We will be equal when?' in one sentence. My answer:

'WHEN THE VIOLENCE STOPS.'

As a positive, glass is half full person it is tough focusing on the negative when women have so much to be proud of and celebrate, but as a modern day feminist I am appalled and ashamed at the unacceptably high levels of violence and exploitation targeted against women and young girls happening all over the globe, every minute of the day and night. I refuse to ignore this and neither should you.

We are living in dangerous times, particularly if you are female. We make up 70% of the world's poorest citizens, we are starving through choice and lack of choice, we are subject to violence, pain, mutilation and death at the hands of those who profess to love us and we are cutting, slicing and scarring ourselves to achieve a deluded version of perfection that is quite simply insane and unattainable. In Africa being born a girl means you are more likely to get raped than learn to read; in China being born a girl increases your chances of being trafficked as boys are prized in a nation where a single child policy is favoured; and if you are a girl conceived in India you are lucky to even be born as an illegal dowry system makes you unaffordable and dispensable and you are just as likely to end up a discarded foetus at the bottom of a disused well.

Here are some facts to get you thinking about what is really going on; it is not easy reading and I would ask you to consider the how and why of the facts. Do we really have equality and respect? Does the sex industry exploit us or empower us?

What does liberation mean to our young girls? Where does the need to inflict pain and disfigure ourselves come from? Could there be a link between the normalisation of pornography and the increase in domestic violence? Why are rape convictions so low? You decide...

Take a deep breath...

There are now more lap dancing clubs (over 300) in the UK than rape crisis centres (only 38). In 2009 the Equality and Human Rights Commission threatened over 100 councils in the UK with legal action because they were failing to provide domestic violence support services or rape crisis centres, despite a growth in incidents reported.

Half of all female murder victims worldwide are killed by a current or former partner. One in four women in the UK will experience domestic violence at some point in her life with two women murdered every week as a direct result (National Crime statistics).

25% of all daily search engine requests are for pornography. 96% of the people doing the searching are male. Every 39 minutes a new pornography video is created in the USA to support this demand. The industry is worth over $97 billion worldwide, more than the combined revenue of Microsoft, Google, Amazon, Yahoo!, eBay, Apple, Netflix and Earthlink.

Global prostitution is growing fast. During the 90s the number of men paying for sex acts in the UK doubled. In 2008 there were at least 921 brothels in London alone.

Between 600,000 and 800,000 people, 90% of them women and girls, are trafficked across national borders every year. Women and girls are trafficked primarily to service the multi-billion dollar commercial sex industry and modest estimates put the income generated by this relatively easy crime at $19 billion a year. Police will tell you this is an invisible, almost impossible crime to detect and is happening on your doorstep every day.

Between 1992 and 2002 the number of people (over 90% female) undergoing elective cosmetic surgery in the USA increased by 1600%. The UK is following the same trend. The most popular procedure in both countries is breast implants, closely followed by liposuction. The latest addition to the menu is 'Designer Vagina' where women elect to have invasive procedures not dissimilar in nature and risk to that which we are outraged about – female genital mutilation. Options include vaginal tightening, liposuction and lifting of lips, clipping of elongated inner lips and 'repair' of the hymen. By this we are saying once the hymen is broken, i.e. when we lose our virginity, we are somehow damaged goods.

Up to 70 million people (mostly women) globally suffer from an eating disorder. 1.5 million of these are in the UK. These disorders are among the top four causes of premature death, illness and disability among women aged between 15-24 years old. 10% of women with anorexia die from it.

94% of all women's magazines have a picture of a model or celebrity on their front cover who would be considered thin, if not clinically underweight. The average model is now thinner than 98% of the female population. The average dress size in the UK is 16, yet a size 12 model is considered plus size. Not surprisingly women are more than 10 times more likely to have issues with their weight than men. In the UK we spend over £11 billion a year on books, magazines, special foods, classes and other aids to weight loss. 95% of all dieters regain their weight loss (Body Image Study for Guardian May 2001 and Body Image Journal 2005 and 2007).

A survey in the UK in 2009 by Youngpoll.com found that a quarter of the 3,000 teenage girls questioned believed it was more important to be beautiful than clever.

The Lab surveyed 1,000 15-19-year-old girls in 2005 about their ambitions; 63% said they would rather be a nude or semi-nude glamour model than a nurse, a doctor or a teacher. This is no better today, the occupation of choice for far too many girls is a reality TV star! Don't even get me started on this one!

Uncomfortable reading, eh? We need to keep asking questions and we need to keep pioneering for a better deal for our daughters. The feminist cause is just beginning. Refuse to be silenced, ridiculed or humoured. Feminism is alive and well, and judging by the number of female-only networks, portals and communities, sisterhood is also on its way back.

CHAPTER FIVE
WOMEN AT WORK – ARE WE THERE YET?

'Until we switch from fixing the women to
fixing the organisations the feminisation
of the workplace is on hold.'

Up until five years ago I spent very little time with professional women since walking away from the corporate world at 28.
Starting out, the focus in the Diva business was entrepreneurship (not so now, many corporate women step up to our programmes, peer groups and coaching) so my instances of working with corporate women were limited to those making the
move into business and therefore in transition. However, my
mission to raise the aspirations of young girls has now brought
me right back into this arena as I encourage big companies to
support our work and harness the talents and passions of these
awesome women to step up and become Big Sister mentors. I
would have to say I am simultaneously in awe of women climbing the corporate ladder today, alongside being completely
frustrated with the environment they inhabit. The slow progress at the top, the endemic sexism, the pay gap, the slow, slow
response to childcare and maternity needs, the appalling pregnancy discrimination and the mass exodus of women from the
sector as they reach middle management.

Where do all the women go and more importantly why?

I am passionate about the need to make corporate UK or corporate global female friendly. Nowadays, I spend many hours
in the company of awesome professional women every week
and I am always amazed by their spirit and frustrated by their
stories, simultaneously. I have been saying we need to stop fixing the women and start fixing the organisations for many years
and still I see little shift in most companies' diversity strategies.

I listened with mixed emotions to a 25-year-old female publishing executive in London recently, as she told me she had to go to her boss and demand a rise because she knew all the men in her office, doing the same job as her, were paid at least £7k a year more. She talked of the embarrassment and humiliation of having to do this but recognised if she didn't she would be failing 'all women'. As a young feminist she talked about 'taking one for the team'.

No doubt, most young women – well, the ones with any aspirations – will enter corporate life excited, with the belief that equality is absolute.

But unless they join a structured graduate or intern programme their starting salary is likely to be lower than their male colleagues' and by middle management many of them will have disappeared as the journey upward becomes less and less attractive. Fuelled by endemic sexism, testosterone-driven values and the clear message that military tenacity is demanded to even consider integrating the role of mother and executive, the choices simply become impossible to juggle and any attempt to live an authentic life is futile.

At the heart of this phenomenon is the loss of female identity and the devaluing of motherhood.

Emily Davison staged her protest and many suffragettes endured horrific hardships to secure women the right to vote, to be heard, to have their say. At no point did any of them express the desire to behave, think or act like men. Equality was fought on the basis of difference, **votes for women.**

Since 2002 the number of women leaving the corporate sector continues to rise and a report by PWC in 2002 confirmed this mass exodus was as high as 40% of senior female talent in organisations across all sectors. This trend is not set to change anytime soon. But are we tackling the real reasons for this exodus? Many of these women have since set up their own businesses or moved into freelance working so they are clearly more than competent and driven, are they not? Being an entrepreneur not only allows some flexibility on hours worked but more importantly it is attractive to smart women as they can steer their own ship, name it, define it and lead by their own values. However, do not be fooled into believing that this is the easy option. Running your own business comes with a different set of challenges. Being your own boss is certainly NOT less hours, less stress or less brain power, but it does allow you to stay true to self, lead from your feminine side without having to justify this and fit your work hours around motherhood. Maybe these benefits give us some insight into why women may be walking away from the corporate world then?

Young women know the journey to the top is tough. They see few role models of women who have done it and done it with ease and even fewer who have arrived at a position of power and also had a family. They still believe they cannot have both. They have working mums, aunts and sisters who have gone before them and their stories are not always pretty. They know the decision to have a family will come up at some point and they know this may be a deal breaker for their career, so many are asking 'why bother?'

The jury is out on the effectiveness of gender-balanced boards but still we debate and debate and while we continue to debate this and women's role in the workplace, the talent pipeline is drying up!

We need to acknowledge that testosterone-fuelled environments, unworkable hours (not the quantity, the set patterns of 14-hour days in the office, the lush hour etc.) and a blasé approach to risk are no longer valued nor prized in business today.

We need to shift from ambition to inspiration, sales to service and competition to collaboration, all truths easier to achieve with women on board. At the moment as women hit the top levels of middle management they have three choices:

1. Go native i.e. behave like a man, become one of the boys, don't rock the boat.

2. Continue to climb and become a trail blazer. This demands focus, a thick skin and highly tuned influencing skills with the acceptance that you will need to switch identities several times a day. It is emotionally exhausting and tough to sustain long term.

3. Get out.

Whilst I continue to salute and champion the women out there making a difference, if we are going to fix the talent leak we need to stop fixing the women and start fixing the organisations.

THE KEY STATS:

The pay gap is 14.5%, rising to 33% in London and 55% in the financial sector. Fawcett Society 2013

Only 17% of all senior jobs in corporate UK are filled by women. Catalyst 2004. A report Bottom –Line: Connecting Corporate Performance and Gender Diversity

Women receive less than half the average bonus men receive. CMI 2012

60% of women in the UK have had a male colleague behave 'inappropriately' towards them. Slater & Gordon 2012

One in eight women have left a job because of sexual harassment. Slater & Gordon 2012

Around 30,000 women lose their jobs each year as a result of pregnancy discrimination (almost 8% of all pregnant women). Equal Opportunities Commission 2005. Since this research was carried out campaigners estimate this figure may have doubled.

Only 3% of women who face pregnancy discrimination seek legal advice. OnePoll 2013

A woman with a child under 11 is 45% less likely to be employed than a man. UK Equalities review 2007.

So all these women become disillusioned and leave, 40% is not a number to ignore surely? So you would think organisations would be researching this and coming up with a better retention strategy, eh? But I see little movement here; the reasons cited for walking away tend to focus around children and the glass ceiling. In other words let's blame the women for not being able to cope, or having other priorities, or not being able to hack it. God forbid there may be something wrong with our organisation or the culture. It has worked perfectly well like this for decades. I agree our childcare provision is unacceptable but I remain unconvinced that women suddenly lose their aspirations and ambitions simply because they give birth. If they did we would not have the growth in Mumpreneurs (hate that term but you know what I mean!) and as for glass ceilings...

THE GLASS CEILING IS FAST BECOMING A RED HERRING

Now, I am not saying I think the glass ceiling is a myth. I just think it is an easy term to cover up some pretty real and important issues going on underneath, some already mentioned. I think it assumes women are not 'good enough' to smash through it and I think this is laughable. For me the question is not why are women not smashing through the glass ceiling, it is why would they want to? We need frame-breaking organisational change to make the world of work female friendly and a shift in the way the media defines female success to make it anywhere near attractive to encourage the next generation to join the party anytime soon.

Our campaigning for parity at the top is no longer just about glass ceilings, it is about empty pipelines too as the talent pool continues to dry up and the corporate sector does very little to empower and equip girls with aspirational hammers.

Teenage girls want to be beauticians, pop stars, glamour models, nursery nurses, nail technicians, and reality TV celebrities at best, and the few who do opt for a more corporate, professional career soon become disillusioned when the job fails to live up to the hype and the ladder becomes impossible to balance everything else on.

How can they be so disinterested in the big jobs, you say? Now, with all the opportunities, the opportunities we have worked so hard to create. How can they shake their head and say no thanks to a career and prefer to stay small, safe and servile?

Well let's review the evidence.

How do the media and the establishment treat women in power? Women in positions of influence? Women at the top? A few recent examples: Professor Mary Beard, the UK's most eminent professor of classics at Cambridge, is vilified for her appearance every time she appears on TV. After her last appearance on BBC Question Time twitter crashed due to the number of shocking comments of a sexist and sexual nature, all focused on her appearance NOT credentials. One tweet even superimposed a picture of a hairy vagina over her face with the tweet 'Would ya'? She has also been called 'too ugly for TV' by one of the UK's leading TV Critics, A A Gill. This unacceptable misogyny sends out very clear messages to impressionable young girls.

Or consider the death threats and brutal treatment aimed at Caroline Criado Perez as she campaigned to stop women being airbrushed out of history by petitioning government to keep a woman on the five pound note. When women dare to step up and project their voice, attempts are made to silence them from all angles, and not just the male-driven media, many women get on the band waggon and vilify them for not having kids; having kids and a nanny; being a workaholic; being single or divorced; behaving like a man or being too feminine and so on… Remember the criticism Sheryl Sandberg got when she published her views on women in work LEAN IN? Not sure I can remember the same abuse directed at ANY man for simply publishing a management book.

So, here is what we are saying to our young girls about the world of work and making it to the top:

'It takes grit, hard work and the tenacity of a pit bull to get to the top. It is full on, men will hate you for it, and so will lots of women. You will have to make huge sacrifices, struggle finding or keeping a husband and your kids; if you get the chance to plan in a career break, it will be a permanent source of grief and guilt. Furthermore, once you get to the top, despite doing the same job as the men in said organisation or industry, the likelihood of you being paid the same or commanding the same respect is doubtful.'

Not inspiring is it? Oh, and lest I forget 'Every decision you make will be put under a gender microscope; you will need to prove yourself over and over and a social life is out of the question.'

If we do not wake up and smell the coffee anytime soon and start sharing our positive, inspiring stories of success to our teenage girls, and/or changing the culture and endemic sexism in the workplace, we can expect more of them to sidestep a career or opt out in their twenties. Doing nothing is a luxury we can no longer afford!

TIME FOR FRAME-BREAKING CHANGE – OUR DAUGHTERS NEED TO SEE, AS WELL AS BELIEVE

I watched the film *Made In Dagenham* recently and jumped off the sofa, cheering at the last scene where the women from the Ford plant stood proud with Barbara Castle, the then Secretary of State (1968) while she announced their victory and the Government's commitment to what was to become the Equal Pay Act of 1970. To think this was 44 years ago and the battle is still not won. Don't get me wrong, I think these women were awesome and watching their fight makes me very proud. It also proves to me, again, how important a unified voice is, as a handful of women became a sisterhood and literally brought the Ford business to its knees. Inspirational stuff.

It also made me think about sisterhood and our voice today. Are we as committed to the campaign for equality in the workplace? Or do we believe the job is done? Do we band together or do we stay quiet for fear of being seen as too demanding or a raving feminist (whatever one of those is)? Have we become a society more focused on individual rights with the mentality of 'I am OK so not going to rock the boat or support others who may not be'?

Personally if I hear one more man announce with furore 'gender parity at the top is no longer a nice to have, it is a business imperative' I will scream. Why? Because I don't believe them! Words are cheap and in most cases the action is sadly lacking. If they truly believed this statement surely they would be taking positive steps to make it happen, the job would be done or well on the way.

The only thing that makes me angrier is to hear women already at the top echo the same sentiments when their organisations are doing little to effect change and banish the unconscious bias still apparent in recruitment and promotion practices across the board.

I recently attended a conference titled 'Diversity – The business case for gender parity' hosted by a leading bank. As the speaker was over an hour late the panel of two senior women and two senior men, all from the bank, facilitated a Q&A session. This was planned for the end of the event but was brought forward to kill time while we all waited for the high-profile speaker to show. This debate highlighted the 'all talk and little action' mentality perfectly. The talk was word perfect but the action was misguided, non-existent and/or flawed.

The senior woman at the bank proudly shared the massive action the bank was taking to close the gap and change the status quo internally: 50/50 gender appointments for graduate entrants; flexible working; recognition of female leadership qualities and companywide training on unconscious bias in recruitment and promotions. Sounded great, eh? Apart from the graduate recruitment, at a time when we have more female graduates than male, this is hardly a coup.

Then came the killer – the male representative at the bank was asked his view on the unique leadership attributes women bring to the table and the bank's credibility took a nose dive. Here was his response. 'Well I see no difference in men and women, successful people are the same. Women do well in xx bank. For example, I have a woman on my team who is bright, good at her job and has been promoted many times and still manages to look after her kids and husband.' So much for unconscious bias training, maybe he was off on that day?!

What was more frustrating was the lack of response from the women on the panel. They did not even blink at his cringeworthy indiscretion, despite the audible intake of breath from the women in the audience. Is this ignorance, apathy or another example of unconscious bias?

I was left wondering if you need to be outside the system to influence and change it. Are we expecting too much from women who have to work within this male indoctrinated culture? Is it too hard to create dissonance with the status quo at the same time as looking after your own career interests?

One of the most important lectures I ever attended as part of my MBA many years ago was on the subject of change in corporate cultures. Forgive me for launching into an academic model but this one helps identify for me what is going wrong.

Apparently there are only two types of change – incremental and frame breaking – and it is imperative to classify the nature of change you are hoping to effect correctly to secure success. Misdiagnosing the type of change can be catastrophic and doom any change programme to failure from day one. All organisations experience both types of change along the way. Incremental change is a permanent fixture for any successful organisation – new customers, IT systems, continuous improvement doctrines etc. but frame-breaking change comes around less often, and when it does the nature of the shifts needed demands focused effort and investment. This is where I think we are going wrong. Equality and changing the culture in organisations is frame-breaking change yet we are attempting to implement subtle shifts and tackle endemic sexism incrementally. This is not working as if you identify frame-breaking change as incremental you give people too much time to subvert the process and we see this happening all the time, particularly by men who want to retain the status quo (in most parts). Frame-breaking change needs strong leadership from the top, it needs powerful role models, men and women of gumption not afraid to step up and speak out. It needs clear targets and accountability and it needs buy-in across the company with real consequences when it is disregarded.

On the flip side, if you identify every change necessary in an organisation as frame breaking this is also a recipe for disaster as people are always in the throes of a 'perceived' major change programme and motivation suffers. Then when the need for real frame-breaking change arrives, and it will, people do not step up, nor do they believe the seriousness of the change as it feels like just another day at the office of permanent change programmes!

It is time for frame-breaking change. Now is the time for courage, focus, gumption, targets and most importantly ACTION. How will we attract the next generation of female leaders without any of this? And how will we take our rightful seat around the top table?

This brings me to the topic of quotas.

QUOTAS – CAN I CHANGE MY MIND?

Recently, I inadvertently ended up in a conversation with an angry bloke about quotas on company boards and why women don't get to the top. He was adamant it is because they don't want to, nor are they qualified or competent enough to, and if we introduced quotas we would end up with women not suitable or capable of the job in hand just to meet some stupid target! Phew, answer that one, Diva! I am sure you know that I did! Like the current system has never promoted a man who was not capable for the job in hand, eh?

However, my view on quotas has gone full circle. If you had asked me how I felt about them 10 years ago I would have been vehemently against such positive action for all the well-reasoned arguments people use today: it will upset the men and alienate them rather than get them on side; it will promote women not ready for the position and thus work against us as opposed to for us; it will be seen as tokenism and the women in question will not be taken seriously, and so on, but today I see the situation very differently so why have I changed my mind?

As a coach and innovator I recognise that some situations need a serious intervention to create dissonance with the status quo and frame-breaking change as I mentioned before. Getting women to their rightful place, sharing the decision-making process in the corporate, political, educational and legal arena is an example of frame-breaking change and this level of change cannot be done incrementally, it demands a serious shift and serious shifts do not happen organically.

Sometimes we have to accept a short-term change to achieve a permanent one and I think introducing quotas for a 30% female board representation is one of those. The quota only needs to be in place until the permanent change is embedded, but without it we are going to keep plodding along making little impact and giving the establishment more and more time to subvert the process.

We know it makes sense to have a more balanced boardroom. The business case is clear: over 80% of all consumer decisions are made by women, women make up over 50% of the population, girls outperform boys academically, blah blah. The evidence is clear but, and it's a BIG but, if we continue doing what we are doing this 30% target will get further and further away from us and what message does this send out to young girls? If they cannot see any women at the top why should they believe it is possible? Action speaks louder than words and if all we ever do is talk about it...?

For those token women out there that are at the top, I salute you! You have worked hard and sacrificed much to get there but is that really the way it should be? Is this the message to our girls? Only a few can succeed and the sacrifices are huge? Tokenism does not work, we need a posse of women or none, the pressure on the lone female is too much and one woman cannot be expected to represent her whole gender in every decision and move she makes.

In my opinion, we have to invade the top in groups if we are to impact the landscape – 30% is a start and to say the talent is not out there? Well the naysayers are definitely not going to the networks I am going to, the talent is bursting at the seams and raring to go. It may not be boasting on the golf course or blagging in the corporate box at the cricket or bigging up the CV at the corporate recruitment shows but it is ready and waving. It is an unnatural female trait to blag and boast, we hope our skillset and readiness for the next position is clear by the quality of our work and outcomes. Unfortunately, as the majority of people doing the recruiting are men we are on different pages and this is a key reason why men think there is no talent and women feel they are either overlooked or somehow not promotion material.

But I suspect something else is going on too. I am not convinced men want us around. I think they are creating some emotional barriers to entry we are buying into to protect their turf. Remember the disquiet around the time of the Great War? Women can step up and run the country doing men's work but only 'for the duration'. Duration is over now and they have been fighting to maintain control ever since. However, when you are the majority, possession is nine tenths of the law so it is not that difficult to do! If we are struggling to calibrate our changing role in society, believe me they are fighting to hold on to theirs too! In simple terms men do not know how to manage, connect and co-exist with women in the workplace and this gets more and more problematic as we climb the ladder. Even if they like having women around they do not want to work for one. You may disagree with this but if they felt secure in sharing this space we would not be in the position we are in now, would we? This is why we need legislation. The alternative is like shifting deck chairs on the *Titanic*. We can tweak the odd hidden rule and wait like 'good girls' but natural evolution may be centuries away, and personally I feel this is too high a risk and too high a price to pay for the next generation.

I also see too many bright women buying into the hype that they are not good enough, or not board ready, or just need some more qualifications, or more confidence etc. I think we have stayed so long in positions where our value is marginalised and our self-esteem has been chipped away at that we have started to believe that we are not worthy of promotion and so the whole 'promotion on merit only' campaign suits us because it allows us to hide, or gives us more time, or feeds into our fear that maybe, just maybe, the men are right and we are not capable of doing the jobs at the top. We have become our own worst enemy. It is ridiculous to believe that quotas would promote incompetent women. There would still be a recruitment and selection process, all quotas would do is make sure the shortlist was gender balanced to give women a fighting chance. What are we afraid of, really?

Unless we change the gender make-up at the top these cultural anomalies will continue to keep women in straightjackets. The time for legislation is now, we need to be brave, stand up and be counted and know that, in the short term, temporary quotas will get us what we want, get us what we deserve and afford the next generation a chance of a more balanced view from the top.

Let's talk about working mums

This section would not be complete without the discussion around women and children. This is a biological issue, is it not? Until men can give birth and opt to do so, the human race will cease unless we keep doing it! But in a society where dual income couples are the norm and since the Great War of 1914 women have been prominent in the workplace, you would think we would have found a better way of managing the inevitable, i.e. women in work having babies.

Many countries have a more shared approach to childcare and maternity/paternity leave where both the man and woman are entitled to six months' leave each to encourage a fairer system for both parents. In Britain and the US we seem to be stuck in the dark ages and regardless of the father's needs, we plant the responsibility for childcare and all it encompasses firmly at the mother's feet. Now forgive me, but I was under the impression that reproduction was a joint affair and although childbirth may be the exclusive domain of women, making kids and raising kids is definitely a together process!

WORKING MUMS – I SALUTE YOU ALL!

How many times have I listened to politicians and business commentators state with passion and conviction how important it is to recruit and retain women in the workforce? How as a nation we are missing out on so much talent and how women are going to be our economic rescue. I so wish I could believe their perfectly written and delivered speeches but sadly I can't. Why?

Well, what we do know for sure is that not only are women not entering the workforce, they are choosing not to return after having children and many are leaving corporate jobs due to lack of flexibility and parity, lack of alignment with personal values, lack of progression, impossible work patterns, endemic sexism and hidden discrimination to name a few reasons.

But the biggest killer of anyone's motivation and incentive must be the lack of reliable and/or affordable childcare for the under-fives. I am astounded at the cost. In my home town, a decent nursery place, if you can get one, for one child can cost between £10-£14k a year. Are you kidding? Where is the incentive to work if it costs this much to put one child in a nursery for a standard 8am-6pm day? As a working mum the guilt and military-style organisation necessary to get back to work is stressful enough but then to know that your childcare is costing as much as your mortgage is not exactly making you feel like you have made the right choice or that your employer values your return. It would be interesting to see how many men would work at the same punishing corporate intensity if we docked their salaries by £14k a year.

Yet we expect working mums to be fully engaged, 100% motivated and just as willing to work out of hours, go the extra mile for promotion and travel as much as the guys, who in 95% of cases do not accept the same level of responsibility for the child. Are we mad or simply deluded?

There are now more women working in Germany, France and the Netherlands than in the UK. This is a complete turnaround from the 1980s when exactly the opposite was true. So ask yourself, what are they doing that we aren't? Better childcare and better work conditions for working parents – it's that simple.

It is time for a rethink. We cannot simply write off working mums, our economy needs them. We have to accept that some women – in fact rather a lot of women – will at some point in their journey give birth, it is the natural order of life, they should not be penalised for it. In order to recoup the investment we need to encourage them back to work, be it as employers or entrepreneurs, and to make this a more realistic and frankly a more attractive option, we need better, more reliable and more cost-effective childcare along with more flexibility in working patterns and more feminine leadership styles. Until we do this, as opposed to talk about it, the rescue is on hold.

We need to stop treating childcare as a female issue. I have never heard of a man being asked at interview if he intends to have a family, or being sidelined when his wife is pregnant, or losing his job once she has the child. The sooner we change maternity leave to family leave and recognise men's role in this process the better. I know many men who would love to spend more time with their kids and would definitely take family leave if it was offered to them. However, I also know many others who would never admit to this for fear of losing face.

I think the pressure we place on women about motherhood is unacceptable.

CAREER WOMEN – HAVE BABIES TO SUIT YOU NOT THE ESTABLISHMENT PLEASE!

Over the past 12 months as I have gathered my thoughts and research together to write this book I have seen several articles in the women's glossies discussing the issue of when we should have babies – post- or pre-career – and I've got to be honest, even the question winds me up!

Maybe I am naïve, uneducated or missing the point but I thought our campaigning for equality was about NOT having to make such arbitrary choices. I was unaware that our biological clocks and reproductive systems have become an acceptable setback to our right to a career and equal footing with men. I understand that men might use this as a barrier to entry but I did not expect women to be spouting the same inane nonsense too! Have we surrendered our power here?

In one magazine two women argue the case for either waiting until you are well into your thirties before getting pregnant versus having your kids while you young – i.e. 'get them out of the way early' as she so eloquently puts it!

The premise of all these articles is if you want kids and a career, you are either going to have to fight your biological clock until your career is bedded in, or don't bother getting on the ladder until you have reproduced. This way when you come back to work in your thirties, ready to rock and roll, lots of your female peers will be dropping out of work to have kids and you will have the advantage. I find both options offensive, sad and hardly an advert for sisterhood.

Incidentally, both these women consider themselves feminists, keen to empower their daughters with their choices. Not sure either opinion is going to empower young girls to even put one foot on the corporate ladder anytime soon. The whole concept of micromanaging your biological clock turns me off and I have never even had kids. Maybe this is the issue? Maybe this is why I don't get it? I am happy to concede this but I have to tell you that convincing the next generation of young women may not be so easy. If we are not creating a world of work where having a family is seen as normal, a joint responsibility and doable we may end up right back where we started with male-dominated workforces and frustrated stay-at-home mums.

So let's not buy into the warped view that we need to control our biological clock and schedule baby making like a long-term goal or our annual appraisal review. For many women, waiting for the perfect moment can be heart-breaking as conceiving in your late thirties is not always a walk in the park.

For me feminism stands for equal rights, to have the same opportunities for advancement as men, and until men evolve to give birth, the world has to accept that women will need time out of work to keep the population going! Caring for and taking responsibility for children must be seen as a joint responsibility and this is the debate we should be having, NOT how do we stay obedient and create as little disruption to our work as possible so we can sneak away and give birth. All feels a tad too subservient for me!

And my final rant on workplace sexism...

I know from my conversations with women there is a lot of denial about the presence of workplace sexism, it is as though if we admit it we will be seen as party poopers, or weak, or ball-breaking feminista! But ignoring it is unwise and selling out. I am not talking about nude calendars or the odd comment about 'time of the month'. I am talking about serious sexual harassment, bullying and blatant exclusion on the basis of gender.

The research confirms we have a problem.

60% of women in the UK have had a male colleague behave 'inappropriately' towards them and one in eight women have left a job because of sexual harassment. This has gone beyond wolf whistling and the odd inappropriate joke. I was saddened then angry at the content of Laura Bates' book *Everyday Sexism*. Laura is a young woman who reached her personal tipping point on sexism in 2012 and set up a twitter account and website inviting women from around the world to share their stories. The response has been mind-blowing and continues to reveal the extent of what seems to have become an invisible, not talked about crisis. Hand on heart this is the most heart-breaking book I have ever read. So much so, I had to read it in stages as I was either in tears or banging my head against the wall in utter frustration by the end of each chapter. I am astounded we have let this happen right in front of our noses and we are too afraid to report this appalling behaviour. I have some sympathy with the female victims here but unless we start stepping up and saying no, and if necessary pressing charges for some of these physical assaults, what messages are we giving the sad, aggressive, predatory males who do this? And before you say not all men are like this, believe me I know that too. But not supporting the women who have and are experiencing sexual harassment simply gives the wrong men even more power. We have to harness our courage and make it stop.

Rather than discuss this, I thought it would be more powerful to share a sample of comments submitted to the project recently.

'Male colleague after putting the phone down to a female client: "I wish I could stick my c**k in her ear and f**k some sense into her". I am not over exaggerating, this kind of thing is an everyday occurrence in my office, along with comments about the size of my breasts.'

'My manager bullied and sexually harassed me over a period of a year. In December last year he grabbed my face with both his hands and licked around my lips as if he was kissing me. I pulled my lips tight together so he could not put his tongue in my mouth. When he released my face I put my face in my hands and said go away. He then said "mop the wet patch up from under your chair woman".'

'I work in a male dominated business environment, every off-site meeting one of my male team members tries to get off with me, last time the director tried to sleep with me, dragging me to his hotel room and leaving finger-shaped bruises on my upper arm for over a week. I didn't report it to HR as I want to get on in my career and I don't want to be sacked.'

'I worked at a top law firm in recruitment and have heard partners assessing female candidates according to their attractiveness.'

'A male professor at a university I used to work at doesn't hire attractive women to work there as he feels it would distract the men from their work.'

'My boss who is in his 40s tried to kiss me after the Christmas party. I am 22. I went to the woman who co-ordinates the graduates and told her what had happened. I was told this was to be expected in an office and if I asked for a move it would affect my future career. So I continued in my position but felt so uncomfortable I would make myself throw up before I met with him.'

'HR manager told me on the first day: "If you are going to report sexual harassment, first think about what you were wearing on that day".'

'I am 18 years old and work as a receptionist in a car showroom. As the only female member of staff I'm forced to endure sexually charged comments on a daily basis from men old enough to be my father. I've complained to my boss (also male) who dismissed it as banter. The message I got from this meeting was if I couldn't handle the situations other workers put me in, then leave.'

'I was raped by a colleague on a work's night out. Guess who lost their job? Not him.'

'A senior adviser to me, while working late during our busiest period of the year: "What are you still doing here? Isn't your boyfriend hungry? He must be getting lonely." A few days later as I am preparing to take some work home with me: "You know, a married woman should never take work home with her. I mean, it's natural for a married man, but a married woman shouldn't be distracted at home".'

'I am in my early 40s, a professional, with a PhD and 15 years' experience. I recently came back from maternity leave to my overseas posting to meet my new boss for the first time. In our first meeting, he explained that I would no longer be in charge of the

unit I had been setting up for a year due to my "special circum-
stances", and because he wanted to make sure that he respected
the rights of my baby to have his mother around. He also stated
that while I was nursing it will be difficult for me to focus on the
job. So he was being generous by giving me less responsibility and
downgrading my position.'

'A guy sat me down to explain why feminism has no relevance in
2013 while stroking my leg the whole time.'

Are you ranting yet? Are you trying hard not to believe this?
Are you confident it does not happen at your place, are you
trying to find a way to blame the victims? Are you convincing
yourself these are isolated incidents and over exaggerated? Believe me when I say this is the tip of the iceberg, and whether
we like it or not, it will not stop until we stand up and fight
back. I know this is tough and feels scary but we need to do
this together and where necessary use the law to effect change.
I love this comment by a young girl on the site:

'A guy at work used to think it was OK to only ever address me
as big boobs, "morning big boobs" etc. I started addressing him
as "small penis" – he soon realised that maybe saying "morning
Kate" would be better.'

Inspired! Play them at their own game, love it!

It is not banter, it is not harmless fun and in many cases it is
tantamount to assault. It also occurs to me it is in the interest of
the good guys to nail these reprobates too, as standing by while
this goes on could be interpreted as condoning it.

Here is a more subtle example that most of us would not even
question:

Well done dear! Changing attitudes is not for the fainthearted!

Patience is not a virtue I possess, so I recognise many of my
frustrations regarding the way women are tolerated in business
is simply because we are still so new at it. I understand we only

have 60 years of being taken relatively seriously under our belt and the Equal Pay Act only came into being in 1970 but I continue to be disappointed and often outraged at the perceptions of some men who STILL believe women should be full-time home makers and mothers ONLY. Everyone is entitled to their opinion but many of these men control our industry, the media, our political landscape and our public sector. At this point their pre-Victorian values and pontificating become an issue for all of us.

I accept we are still learning to play the game and striving to be taken seriously but sexism is endemic and quite often so subtle it goes unnoticed and unchallenged. Here is an example that raised my temperature recently.

On the drive home from the city the other day I was listening to BBC local radio's coverage of the region's Inspirational Women Awards 2012. The winners were interviewed by a male host (?) as they left the stage holding their trophy. The winner of the media category was the first woman ever to hold the position of editor of a pretty well-known and reputable regional newspaper. The host patronised her for a few moments then went in for the kill by asking her if she was a mother. When she answered yes he then responded, and I quote: 'Wow, you must find it tough to manage such an important, high-profile job with being a mother and caring for your family. How do you do this?' At this moment my heart sank, but I remained hopeful that she would answer with confidence, certainty and a touch of indignation at the relevance of the question. I was disappointed but not surprised by her answer.

She delivered the script many women do when faced with this blatant sexism. She expounded the saintly qualities of her very patient and supportive husband and expressed her gratitude and appreciation of her daughter who put up with her neglect as she sneaked into the back row of the school plays, always late and only had quality time to share with her at weekends. Arrgh! Why do we do this to ourselves?

The interviewer oohed and aahed his way through her reply and finished with the classic 'But do you think they will both be proud of you today?' Translated as 'Maybe they will forgive you for your constant neglect because now you can show them you are good at your job'!

Some of you will argue that he was not sexist in his approach, he was simply asking real questions that women want to know the answer to. I disagree, I subscribe to another classic Caitlin Moran definition of equality here, i.e. it is sexist behaviour if the same questions/approach is NOT acceptable to both sexes. So in this instance, would the interviewer have asked a man just picking up an award for excellence the same question: 'So Bob, well done on your award, are you a father and how do you manage to balance your career with caring for your family?' No No NO, I think not!

Sometimes, in fact quite often, sexism lies just under the surface and it becomes so endemic we barely notice it let alone challenge it, but if we continue to walk around with our eyes closed and think we are rising above this attitude, we are in denial and nothing will change and we will only have ourselves to blame when we look behind and our daughters are NOT following us.

WOMEN IN SUITS – IT IS TIME TO UNITE!

I implore you to keep up the good fight and come together in unity to make the world of work a safe and inspiring place for us and our daughters. Together we are stronger and now is the time for sisterhood not sister baiting. We need to hold fast to our authentic self, accept no compromise, own our choices, dump the superwoman cape and empower each other to be real, to be present and to be feminine. To embrace our emotional heart, to invest in our personal brand and inject corporate UK with a massive and sorely needed dose of feminine common sense and energy!

We need to be kinder to ourselves and each other and tougher on those who hurt us, exploit us, marginalise us and disrespect us.

We need to ensure organisations stop 'fixing' women and start fixing the organisational weaknesses and testosterone-fuelled cultures and we must speak up to put an end to workplace sexism. All of this demands courage and gumption but we have an abundance of this, and our sisters who came before us who were imprisoned, abused and cast out of society for even asking need us to do this. The fight is not over.

JUST ASK, AND ASK NOW!

If there was ever a time to stop and ask, it is NOW:

- Ask for promotion
- Ask for a pay rise
- Ask for action against sexism
- Ask your sisters for support
- Ask for that investment
- Ask for a seat around the table
- Ask for a mentor
- Ask for more help running the home
- Ask for childcare support
- Ask for the sale

Too many times we expect everyone around us to be professional mind readers and simply know what we need or what we feel needs to happen next and so we wait patiently. We know we are capable of and need promotion; we know we do too much at home; we know we should be paid more; we know we are in the wrong job or the wrong business but we need to stop assuming everyone else has got our back and accept that our life plan is exactly that – OURS – and no one else is going to make it happen.

So my message is simple.

Stop waiting for permission to shine; stop sitting pretty with your fingers crossed hoping someone will recognise your brilliance; STOP PLAYING SMALL; stop expecting others to make room for you at the table; stop believing that doing a good job will secure an automatic promotion; stop with the delusion that men want a clean and tidy house. Sorry, that one may be just me! I believe men have domestic dyslexia but I may have been hoodwinked on that one!

The life you have today is only the result of what you did and believed yesterday and the day before and the day before that so you can change it in an instant, you just have to believe and take action.

The world is shifting. Feminisation of leadership, business and politics is peeking around the corner and we need to get ready, we need to embrace our female power and know for certain we deserve equal opportunities and we are more than capable of rocking it!

If we do not do this what are we teaching the next generation? Their choices will simply diminish and everything we have pioneered for over the past 150 years will be wasted.

Do I need to chain myself to some railings anytime soon? Please don't make me!

So step up, take responsibility, ASK and take action!

PART FIVE
OUR TEENAGE GIRLS ARE IN CRISIS

'In school today the most important currency is your "hot monitor". Girls will exchange anything and everything for validation about their appearance.'

CHAPTER ONE
INTRODUCTION

We have arrived. The motivation behind my words, the stories, the pleas, the lessons. The journey so far has brought us to this point, the driving force for my passion, the focus of my legacy, the end game. To raise the aspirations of teenage girls who are struggling to shine growing up in our misogynist society, where your 'hot monitor' is more prized than your intellect; where your sexuality is judged by porn imagery; where every decision and choice you make is broadcast to the world via social media and where you are likely to be in the middle of a full-on identity crisis before you hit 15!

The landscape our girls are growing up in is harsh. My goal is that by the end of this book you will share my fire to change their world and step up and become a role model, engage in our cause and support the work of Girls Out Loud. I also hope for the mothers, sisters, aunts and grandmas among you that this knowledge will help you to understand their world a bit better and encourage you to show them a better way.

Now, when I challenge you to step up and become role models, I also suggest this is not an automatic status for us all. Being a role model intimates you are getting your life vaguely right, as opposed to precisely wrong; it suggests your choices are inspiring others; that you are an advocate and shining example of success in your industry/sector and that the messages you project are positive and authentic. In other words, young girls are looking at you and saying 'You know when I grow up I want to be just like Jane, she rocks' as opposed to 'You know when I grow up, I am definitely NOT doing what Jane does, I am going to marry a footballer instead!'

My definition of a role model is simple:

1. You are comfortable in your own skin.

2. You can define your own success.

3. You are committed to sharing your journey and time with young girls to help them find their voice and un-cover their greatness.

I am hoping that once you get to the end of this section you will know what to do in your heart.

CHAPTER TWO
GIRLS IN CRISIS – REALLY?
'Denial is futile and keeps us stuck.'

I started to get pretty antsy about what I was seeing and hearing about teenage girls around 2007. After several red flags and the opportunity to speak in many schools I decided to dedicate the next act of my life to helping girls find their voice and step up and shine. The past five years since launching Girls Out Loud has been one hell of a ride. It has been emotional, shocking and inspirational. At the beginning I had no idea how damaged our girls were, how destructive and harmful their landscape had become, or how much they were crying out for role models to show them a better way. In the past five years their world has become harder to navigate as the pressure intensifies and I would be doing them a disservice if I did not tell you what it is like being a girl today. The stats will shock you, their stories will upset you and some of their views will make you want to SCREAM. But this is their world and we cannot change their view unless we acknowledge where they are and how they got here.

As a modern day, career-focused businesswoman I celebrate our emancipation and I always assumed my success would be surpassed by the next generation with ease. What I see every day, regardless of social background, is girls playing it safe for fear of being seen as too demanding or unattractive to boys; opting out of careers as it appears too hard – there don't seem to be many women that make it and even fewer with kids so opting for any easier route and waiting to start their own family seems preferable; girls so consumed with their appearance everything else fades into the background and they cut themselves, starve themselves and discount themselves totally while trying to look like a living doll; girls sexually active at 14 but ill-equipped emotionally to handle the fallout and poorly educated on the issue of consent, respect, personal boundaries and safety; girls afraid of standing out and being perceived as different; girls getting trapped in the social media web of show and tell; angry girls screaming in pain at their sexual exploitation, but no one is listening.

I have had many conversations with women about the state of play here, only to hear the response 'Yeah, well it is no different to when we were kids, the teenage years are always difficult.'

Whilst I recognise the sentiments here I absolutely dispute the similarities. To be honest, when I was 15 I was in love with David Cassidy, reading Jackie magazine and wanted hair like Donna in 4F. Yes I had body hang-ups but they revolved around getting into my size 10 two-tone jeans while lying on the bed brandishing a coat hanger; no starving was required, nor did I have to contend with the internet, mobile phones, porn, a sick media, sexual grooming, STDs, drugs or sexting, so let's get real!

Even relatively young women are struggling to comprehend the world of teen angst today. My daughter Holly is only 25 and her jaw drops just as fast and as far as mine in casual conversations with girls in schools nowadays.

I see a generation of vulnerable, disengaged, angry, confused, lost and troubled girls and I cannot sit on the sidelines and watch. What I have come to realise through my work is that these girls are crying out for guidance but our education system is ill-equipped to give them what they need. They need role models not simply academic targets. They need real women with real stories to help them find their voice. They need personal attention and often a serious intervention to understand the choices they are making as the peer pressure is so intense; breaking away from the crowd takes courage and they are sadly lacking in this. They need emotional resilience, a trait they are being denied as the concept of failure is not up for discussion nor is it tolerated in many schools and they need more focus on social and life skills, an area even the best schools fall short on in terms of financial resources and in-house expertise.

I know at this point you will be shouting at me with indignation saying 'Well, my daughter is in a good school, one I pay a lot of money for her to attend, so although I can understand this may be the picture in tough, inner city schools, my daughter is safe.' Think again. Money will not protect her from a sexist society, or the media onslaught, or the internet. I have worked with girls across the board and I am sorry to report many of the issues around appearance, self-harming, eating disorders, confidence, sexuality, anxiety, depression, low aspirations and identity are all the same. They may look different at first glance but they are all rooted in the same motives.

ACADEMIC PROWESS IS NO SUBSTITUTE FOR EMOTIONAL RESILIENCE

One of the motivational sessions I ran exclusively for girls was at a top academic all-girls school with a national reputation for excellence. After my talk a painfully shy girl approached me and said she was depressed and a bit lost as to what she was going to do when she left school. I asked her what she wanted to do and what she loved and she told me music was her passion but because she had only achieved a B grade in her mocks she had to drop the subject. This kind of pressure can trigger a myriad of mental health issues to say nothing of sabotaging her future happiness. These kinds of schools breed a competitive spirit which I can see has benefits for many but leaves others behind. I have met so many girls in their twenties who had this level of education and were pushed into professional careers because this was felt to be the right thing and the preferred route, or they were following in the footsteps of successful parents. I have also coached many of these girls when they hit their late twenties and know for sure they are on the wrong path. In the same way girls from poor, working class or welfare parents struggle daring to suggest they want to go to university; girls from wealthy, middle class parents struggle to suggest they don't want to go. This is the same issue, different manifestation. Both are about not having the confidence, resilience and courage to plough their own furrow.

Let's remind ourselves of some of the key stats:

1. 47% of teenage girls feel the pressure to look attractive is a disadvantage to being a girl. This figure rises to 76% for 15/16-year-olds. This affects self-esteem, alienates girls who dare to be different and has a huge impact on aspirations.

2. By the age of 10 over 80% of all girls in the classroom will be monitoring their food intake in some way. Many will be actually dieting, starving themselves or using other stimulants to fight off hunger.

3. 87% of teenage girls are now unhappy about their body shape, with girls as young as five worrying about their weight.

4. One in four teenage girls will self-harm in some way before they leave school. This is often a symptom of point 1 but can also be family stress, exam anxiety or boyfriend issues. This harming includes cutting, burning and biting themselves.

5. 5% of girls aged 12-17 are now prescribed antidepressants.

6. There has been a 12% rise in under-16-year-olds with drink-related problems. Six children a day will be admitted to hospital with drink-related issues. Binge drinking is more prevalent among girls and 25% of girls aged 15-16 admit to binge drinking at least once a week.

7. Boys as young at 11 are now addicted to internet porn. This has a negative effect on girls as expectations on how to look and what constitutes normal sex are warped.

8. Girls are now three times more likely than boys to suffer with depression and anxiety attacks.

9. Grooming and sexual exploitation is now commonplace in most towns and girls are now initiated and forced to be active in recruiting.

10. The UK still has the highest teenage pregnancy rate in Europe. It has plateaued over the past few years but it is still unacceptable high.

11. We are seeing a growth in the number of sexually transmitted diseases being diagnosed and for the first time in decades syphilis is back on the watch list.

12. Drug use among young people continues to grow with pot smoking close to becoming an epidemic and an alternative to alcohol for many girls aged 14-18.

13. The issues around early sexualisation and the internet just keep getting worse. The latest trend, sexting, involves girls sending nude/semi-nude pictures of themselves in response to demands from boys who then bribe them with disclosure for more sexual favours. Girls are under more and more pressure to do this as it is now perceived as normal behaviour.

14. One in three girls aged 16-18 have experienced unwanted sexual touching at school.

15. 33% of girls aged 13-17 have experienced some form of
sexual abuse.

16. One in two boys and one in three girls think it is sometimes OK to hit a woman or force her to have sex.

Sources include NSPCC; All-Party Parliamentary Group
(APPG); Bliss magazine; YouGov; Zero Tolerance, Girlguiding
UK; World Health Organisation and Forward.

CHAPTER THREE
EARLY SEXUALISATION – THE LEGACY

*'Sex is a commodity you exchange
for popularity and acceptance.'*

There is no need to debate whether our girls have a body image issue, you can see from the stats it is a problem of huge proportions (no pun intended). Girls are fixated on being skinny. Working with a normal UK size 10, 15-year-old girl recently, I asked her what she wanted, what were her hopes and dreams for the future. Her reply: 'To be heroin chic and have a boob job at 17.' Now for those of you who are not 'down with the kids' heroin chic means as skinny as a drug addict! You do not have to look much further than the mainstream media to see the source of her ambitions; have we or have we not glamorised drug abuse? The never-ending media coverage of Peaches Geldof's death from an overdose is a case in point, or consider how we are bewitched by the modelling industry where a high percentage of catwalk models use drugs to stay stick thin. Even girls that are clever perceive being clever is not enough. 'You gotta be clever and hot and hot generally translates into thin!'

The brilliant Miss Representation campaign in the US states the number one wish for girls aged 11-17 is to be thinner, in fact I defy anyone to find a single girl under the age of 18 without body hang-ups. How utterly distressing – in a world where they can be, do and have anything they put their minds to, all they want is to be skinny!

I see this all the time in my work in schools; however, I also know for sure most girls are struggling to achieve this skinny body and recognise at an intellectual level this is not attainable. It's as though they have to be vigilant and make sure they are not seen to eat, so they attempt to starve all day but I know they are hungry. Whenever I run sessions for girls I always provide refreshments. This may be fruit and nuts, chocolate or as a keen baker I may bring them some homemade goodies as a treat. I have to tell you there is never a single crumb left! It is as though I have given them permission to eat, they feel safe because it is all women together and no one will judge them. But their conversation is littered with references to being thinner, or feeling prettier and the preening never stops. They are constantly messing with their hair, reapplying make-up, rearranging their clothes for maximum impact, exchanging fashion tips, practising their pouts – I kid you not!

And this body fixation is starting to manifest younger and younger. At around four years old, the toys and magazines little girls are steered towards are hardly aspirational. It seems the only characters of note are princesses. Now I would not have a problem with princesses if they were brave and gutsy and came in all colours, shapes and sizes, but alas well over 90% of the images are thin, with pneumatic boobs, porcelain skin, blonde hair, blue eyes and a lovely submissive disposition! If you think I am exaggerating look at the magazine shelf next time you are in a supermarket. I did and once my eyes readjusted to the sea of pink on display I counted at least nine magazines with princess in the title – Tinker Bell, Princess Kingdom, Fairy Princess, Pretty Princess, Disney Princess – do I need to go on? And again the content is dismal – the focus is on weddings, being swept away by a prince in shining armour to a life of servility. The only alternative to this stuff is the lovable Dora the Explorer and a baking magazine. What concerns me is these magazines are targeting 4-6-year-olds and the free gifts include pink lipstick or jewellery. Erm, not sure? And don't get me started on the new franchise for tweens called Monster High – look it up online, I dare ya!

And then they grow up, too fast. By age nine the magazines targeting our girls have taken a more sexual turn, leading with headlines like 'Mascara alone is not enough' or 'The Fight against Cellulite'. Are you sure? By age 13 the magazines of choice are the standard glossy crap millions of girls are reading like Heat, Now, Reveal etc. And I challenge anyone to find anything positive in that junk.

So this stereotyping of women as sexual objects, prized for their beauty and Barbie doll appearance starts at age four and is generally out of control by age nine and then never stops. It follows us through school, university and into the workplace. It is present in our political process, on TV, in the lyrics of the songs we listen to, in the outlook of our role models etc.

Now, I am not simply talking about appearance here. Girls are also picking up cues from the media and society about their role, how to behave and their worth. The magazines are full of articles and headlines focused on women bitching about other women; celebrities with husbands that beat them up but that's OK; women who accept the blame when their husbands cheat on them; beautiful women who cannot get or keep a man because they are too demanding or too successful; women in power who are constantly critiqued for what they are wearing and how they look rather than their influence and intellect; how important it is to stay looking young for as long as possible regardless of the dangers of cosmetic surgery and if it goes wrong we can all have a laugh at your expense anyway; the necessity to be a yummy mummy and lose any baby fat instantly; and working women are blamed for all of society's ills including the low literacy rate of our kids to wandering husbands and the national debt!

The message is clear: your role here is to focus on looking good in order to attract a man. Once you have this man you must stay focused on the task of holding on to your youth and him for as long as you can breathe. You must not let anything get in the way of this, be it a career, your intelligence, friends, giving birth, or raising his children. If you do, then expect to be alone, depressed and unhappy.

And let me just say a few words about teen pregnancy. Although figures in the UK have plateaued we still have the highest teen pregnancy rate in Europe and it seems to me the pressure on contraception and/or parental responsibility is weighted far too heavily on the girls.

TEEN MUMS WITH INVISIBLE TEEN DADS?

In the past few weeks I have been seduced by the TV programme Midwives as it comes on straight after my guilty pleasure The Great British Bake Off. Last week the story of a 16-year-old first-time single mum got me thinking that despite 100 years of liberation and fighting for the right to control our reproductive system, we are still slaves to our biology.

Here was an all too typical scenario of a 15-year-old getting pregnant and not even realising until she was seven months gone so only having a short time to come to terms with the huge shift about to take place in her life. The question of contraception was dismissed and the boy was nowhere in sight. The responsibility for caring and financing this situation now fell to her mum, also a single mum who was also a teen mum, and no doubt us, the State.

It was impossible not to feel this young girl's fear at the situation she now found herself in. School had to come to an abrupt end, her future was uncertain, she was now responsible for this whole other life even before she really knew what she wanted to do with her own. The scene where she talked about feeling depressed after giving birth because all her friends were preparing for their end of school prom that she could not go to was heart-breaking.

Whilst this is becoming an all too familiar theme in our society, what strikes me is the lack of parental responsibility we demand or even ask of the boys. At no point in this story was he mentioned. It was assumed he was not involved and the full burden was automatically hers to deal with. Now I am not suggesting they move in together and are forced into a relationship they clearly did not even have in the first place, but where is the responsibility factor? Are we saying it is OK for boys to go around impregnating girls because there are no consequences?

I cannot tell you how many conversations I have had with teen girls who tell me boys categorically refuse to wear condoms because they don't like them so it is left to them to take full responsibility for contraception or risk pregnancy. Not sure what happened to the word no or f*** off then? And in today's so-called equal society how have we have even allowed ourselves to set it up this way?

The contraception they talk about is either the pill, the patch or the implant – all of which are hormone related and may well create health problems for them in later life. Their young bodies are not ready for this harsh intervention, but I accept it is better than an unwanted pregnancy. However, what about the boys?

What do we do about the boys? If we as a society allow them to believe that unprotected sex is OK and getting girls pregnant is responsibility free, we are taking several giant leaps back on our journey towards empowerment.

Whatever happened to male contraception? I understand the trust issues here, no good developing a pill. My husband cannot even remember if he closed the freezer door or where he left his glasses so I get the concerns around him remembering to take a pill or us even believing he remembered! Surely we need to invest in other methods. Personally I would like to see a male implant developed that is positioned in clear view (forehead, nose or Adam's apple) that flashes green when he is in the safety zone! No room for doubt there, eh?

But seriously, why can't we develop an implant or a patch for boys that girls can see? Failing this technology ever making it to the market in my lifetime, at what point do we make the boy's parents take some responsibility for the babies he creates? The girl's parents have no choice but to support her and the child. It feels unfair that the boys simply carry on as usual.

Now, before you reply telling me the positive stories where this does happen, I know there are some responsible young adults out there, male and female, and I also know mistakes happen. Unfortunately these stories are not presented by our media and therefore do not become the norm. We show girls the opposite story and they accept this as their lot. We let boys continue to behave irresponsibly and this becomes their legacy. All our story lines on soaps, all the scenarios on reality TV, all our press stories etc. focus on the young, teen, single, first-time mum – scared, alone and living with mum.

And let me just rant about reality TV for a moment, the scourge of teen girls everywhere. Kim Kardashian is one of the most popular role models mentioned by girls in UK classrooms from age 12 up at the moment – they think she is naturally beautiful (?), clever, rich and successful. She has everything they aspire to: hot looks, money, a rich husband, a family and fame. They fail to see the downside of this self-made, fake TV persona, they seem only able to view everything through image-tinted glasses so even when she attracts some bad publicity for bum implants or marriage problems they still love her and want to be her!

RAISING GIRLS – THE TV SHOCKER

By now we are starting to understand that early sexualisation, mainstreaming porn, the internet, the media onslaught about how to look and reality TV have all played their part in where we are, but girls are big business and making them feel bad about the way they look as early as possible is cash in the bank for so many organisations it is simply too tempting to resist. Skincare, cosmetic surgery, the media, make-up, haircare, beauty industry, clothing industry, the toy manufacturers – they all play on exploiting girls so the only question they feel necessary to answer is 'How do I look and am I hot?' In fact the hotness monitor is on overdrive wherever you look.

If the magazines, the internet and Bratz dolls are not destroying our teen girls' egos enough then what they are watching on TV will delete what little self-esteem they have left. Reality TV features the most watched programmes, supposedly about real life but really set-up scenarios where attractive girls and boys are shown having sex, getting off their face on drink, drugs and getting hurt both physically and, more uncomfortably, emotionally. Girls are hooked on these programmes and for them it is more than entertainment, it is a monitor for what is normal and cool and we wonder why they are in the throes of a full-on identity crisis before they hit 16.

Researchers have found that reality TV has six key messages for girls. Take a deep breath…

1. Your looks are the most important thing about you.

2. Your physical characteristics (shape, weight, skin, hair, teeth, colour, smell) are NEVER, EVER good enough.

3. Sex is primarily a currency that you exchange for love, attention and power.

4. It is normal to have sex with people you don't even know or especially like.

5. The world is a scary, lonely, dangerous and competitive place. Better get going – you might lose the race.

6. The answer to all life's problems is to buy something.

Source: Survey Girls Scouts Research Institute 2011

How utterly depressing is that? I reckon this affects girls well past their teen years. I have met several young women in their twenties displaying this life philosophy too.

WHERE ARE THE TOYS?

And if the magazines, TV and web portals don't depress you the toy shelves will. Girls are pink, boys are blue. Girls like to play house, hoover, cook, iron, shop and put on make-up and pretty dresses to get boys' attention, whilst boys like to fight, explore, mess with science, learn about dinosaurs and the planet, get messy and make lots of noise. Now I know in isolation playing house or wanting to be like mummy and baking or ironing is not on its own damaging. I remember having most of these toys but I got bored of them very quickly and much preferred to dance, play on the rope swings in the local quarry with girls and boys, ride my bike, rollerskate or use my imagination in role play to become a teacher, post office owner, international PA or a librarian! The major difference today is I was not surrounded by images and messages telling me how I was supposed to look, what I was supposed to weigh, how I was supposed to dress and walk and have my hair etc. etc. In fact I cannot remember even looking in a mirror or caring about what I put on in the morning on my way out to play and there's the word PLAY. Play was the key thing and lasted right up to when I discovered boys had a little more to offer than the best bike or a bag of marbles! I reckon I was around 12 when this hit home and at this point I was kinda interested in attracting their attention so I made a little effort in my appearance. But make-up? Hair extensions? False eyelashes? Fake tan? Teeth whitening? False nails? Boob jobs? Nose jobs? Provocative outfits? I was still a little girl, living in a society that allowed me to explore my sexuality in my own time and at my own pace. The pressure to grow up fast is on today and we only have ourselves to blame for mainstreaming adult messages to children. Today by age 12 most girls are well aware of their place in a misogynist society where their prime currency is their appearance, being sexy and being obedient.

Here is a comment from a seven-year-old girl: '*Girls have to be pretty but boys don't have to worry too much about what they look like because they are clever and will get a good job anyway.*'

CHAPTER FOUR
TAKING PORN OFF THE TOP SHELF
WAS A HUGE MISTAKE

Now here is a subject very few women like talking about but, unfortunately we cannot talk about the early sexualisation of a generation without discussing how we have allowed the $97 billion (and growing) porn industry to steal and corrupt the sexual development of our kids. The game changed when the internet was born and we have failed to put the filth back in the box ever since.

Today we have boys as young as 11 addicted to porn, and girls queuing up to be porn stars. A new porn film is made every 39 minutes and online in seconds to fuel a massive demand. At the last count, 25% of all daily search engine requests were for porn and 96% of the people doing the searches are male. We have no idea how many of these are boys.

Source www.safetynet.org.uk

We have a problem.

This porn is infecting our children's view of sex and intimacy. It is where and how they get their sex education and as we all know porn has never been particularly empowering for women. It is a fantasy world, created in the main by men, for men. It is not a documentary, nor is it a sex manual. But how are boys to know this when the subject is taboo and no one ever talks about it in or out of school? To view women through this filter is not only damaging in the long term for both boys and girls when they arrive at a point when they are ready for a more permanent relationship based on more than sex, it is also de-personalising the most personal act of all.

Gone are the days of fumbling behind the bike shed or gentle sexual awakenings; the curtains do not open slowly revealing the journey bit by bit anymore. Porn is like a fast-track blind, one yank and it's up and all out on display (forgive the pun) and the personal exploration is over as the imagery makes it clear what you do, when, to whom and how.

As John Bishop, the popular UK comic says when trying to explain the facts of life to his son who had more than likely been watching porn for years: 'To be honest son, women are not always that enthusiastic and they very rarely bring a friend!'

You may be wondering at this point where our kids are watching this porn. Generally on smart phones, where parents seem to have no control. Research by YouGov in January 2012 found nearly nine out of 10 children had no security settings on their phones and only 46% of parents were aware that they were even necessary.

They can also access it online, on Facebook or Snapchat and go into any mixed secondary school at break time and it's not just the girls that are attached to their mobiles phones. Also this imagery is not just seen in porn films, it is everywhere from TV ads, billboards, music videos, the internet, social media and so on. There is no escape unless you live on Mars or in a nunnery.

Porn is easy to download – it is accessible, instant and often free and has become as much a part of their daily banter as grabbing a can of Coca-Cola from the vending machine, and although it may be fun for the guys it sees women subjugated, humiliated and in many cases hurt.

PORN – the gift that keeps on giving

Take this permanently sexually charged environment, add the media, early sexualisation of girls and endemic sexism and it all adds up to misogyny on a grand scale. Boys may be lost but girls are being hung out to dry. Here are some of the challenges we are facing:

1. Many by-products of porn are making it into mainstream culture – body piercings, waxing, tattoos, pumped-up lips, pole dancing, breast and bum implants, big hair, fake tanning.

2. Compounded by lack of relevant sex education, girls are confused on the issue of consent. They don't seem to be able to define rape. Is it rape if I am drunk? Is it rape if I change my mind? Is it rape if I am asleep, or if I have led him on or if I wear sexy clothes? Do I have to have sex with my boyfriend if he wants it? They seem to think it is their fault somehow if they are assaulted. This scene is played out all the time in porn films.

3. The word rape has entered the language of youth in the most inappropriate way. Boys use it simultaneously as a term of endearment and an insult – e.g. 'she is hot I would rape her' versus 'if you don't shut it I will rape you'. Areas of the school playground hidden from CCTV are referred to as 'rape corner'. This intensifies at university (discussed later). A few quotes from women writing in to the Everyday Sexism project below highlight more:

    a. 'I overheard my 13-year-old brother and his pals discussing girls in their class in three categories: frigid, sluts or would like to rape.'

    b. A girl in Year 11 distressed as her school prom was having 'a biggest rapist award' and 'biggest slut award'. The mind boggles...

4. Boys for the most part refuse to wear condoms. It is felt to be uncool so most of them feign an allergy. This means contraception is the girl's responsibility and although many of them are on the pill, have an implant or wear a patch, they still believe 'safe sex' means protecting yourself from getting pregnant. This is partly

responsible for the growth in STD. You never see men wearing condoms in porn films.

5. I cannot tell you how many conversations I have had with 15/16-year-old-girls in relationships who are worried and scared about some of the sexual demands of their boyfriends, often older than them but not always. They are not sure they can say no to these demands which include oral sex where the man ejaculates in their mouth or over their face or body; anal sex; fisting; violent positioning including being tied up and/or temporary asphyxiation; filming the act or inviting others to watch or participate; role playing involving rape and so on. All of these sexual activities should be open to choice, no one should feel pressured to do any of them, least of all teenage girls discovering their sexuality for the first time. It is heart-breaking.

6. Sex is now seen as a commodity not an intimate act. Both girls and boys are not concerned about the number of sexual partners they clock up, compounded by reality TV programmes like The Magaluf Weekender; Sun, Sex and Suspicious Parents; Geordie Shore and so on.

7. The use of derogatory name-calling of girls lifted directly from the porn industry like slut, whore, bitch, hoe, hooker. In a recent survey 71% of girls admitted being referred to in this way by boys and girlfriends.

8. Both girls and boys are sexually active at a much younger age these days. Our 17 is now their 14.

Can I stop now? Please don't tell me this is what it was like when you were a teenager, unless you were a teenager in the past 10 years. This stuff is hard to listen to and even harder to absorb but it is real, it is happening and it is not going away anytime soon. And by the way, the words love and intimacy are sadly missing from most of these conversations, sex is the currency and this is tragic.

We cannot protect them from porn and the rest, it is out there, but we can educate them better and encourage them to talk about this stuff, because believe me they want to talk about it; they are confused, lost and not sure where to turn. According to data collected by YouGov for the End Violence Against Women Coalition, 40% of 16-18-year-old-girls said they did not receive lessons or information on sexual consent, or didn't know whether they had or not. And when Everyday Sexism carried out an informal online poll asking people whether their school sex and relationship education had covered issues such as sexual violence, domestic violence, assault or rape, more than 92% said none of these issues were raised. We need to update our sex education to equip our young for the world they are growing up in and we need to do it now.

CHAPTER FIVE
THE NEW FRIENDSHIP RULES –
LOVE YA BABES!

'This unhealthy intensity of friendships is a symptom of fear.'

I know peer pressure has always existed – hey, it changed my life so you don't have to tell me the extremes people will go to to be seen as cool but something far more intense is playing out, particularly among girls, and I have no doubt it is related to all the things I have talked about so far in this chapter.

School is more in keeping with a nightclub these days – the parading, fashion statements, stimulants, the smoking, sexual predators, groping and sexual advances and so on. Some girls manage this environment well and others spend every day living in fear. The latter group are terrified of walking past a group of boys, won't do PE or even take their blazer off in 80 degree heat due to the intensity of their self-consciousness and body hatred. These girls have what appear at first glance to be very unhealthy relationships with other girls. They are inseparable. They wear exactly the same attire in the same way, choose the same options, speak in stereo and find it hard to function without each other. They sit in comfortable silence stroking each other and playing with each other's hair like chimps, I kid you not! You could be forgiven for believing their love for their best friend is more than platonic as they scream 'love ya babes' every time they meet or leave each other even for a minute! I have seen this played out many times and spoken to bemused teachers about this growing trend in many schools.

The other group of girls appear tough, streetwise and sassy. They bat off the guys' sexist behaviour and strut around school like supermodels, pouting, hitching their skirts up as far as is decently acceptable and copying the facial expressions they see on pop videos every day – thanks Rhianna! They know all the language, the slang and are addicted to their mobile phones. They text and message each other all the time, even in class, are more likely to be the smokers and recreational drug users (mainly pot) and are most definitely sexually active.

The thing is, both these groups of girls are vulnerable and not sure how to behave. They are acting out roles to protect themselves and sometimes it works and sometimes it fails. When you get into rapport with them and peel back the layers they are just scared girls trying to navigate their way through a myriad of daily decisions about the way they look, their hot monitor, boys, sex, girlfriends, ever changing peer groups, bad behaviour and anger and they are generally doing this on an empty stomach, surviving on little more than a couple of cans of pop and a packet of crisps a day. These decisions take precedence over school work, exam prep, career planning, homework etc. There go their aspirations then, eh?

Their friendships are more intense and yet simultaneously emotionally deficient when you experience how quickly they can banish friends from their peer group. They are inseparable one week and hating each other the next. Their need for complete trust and loyalty is a little daunting for their age and again this is born from fear. I have seen girls be totally in love one week and arrived to deliver a group session the next and they refuse to participate because X is in the room. It is bizarre and exasperating but it is their norm. Their hatred for one another quickly turns vitriolic and often it is impossible to get to the bottom of why. The name-calling is horrific, back to point 7 above and the concept of forgive and forget has been forgotten long ago.

All of this is painful to observe. They are angry and let's be honest, who wouldn't be, having to put up and shut up in this way? They are confused as to how they are supposed to behave in a world that encourages and positively baits them to be sexy, dress sexy, behave sexy then vilifies them for their own exploitation if anything untoward happens to them i.e. it's her own fault, she was asking for it, her shorts are too short, she looks like a hooker, she should not have been drinking late at night, she should not have walked home on her own, she should have said no etc. etc. This double bind has girls cutting themselves, starving themselves, medicating themselves and in rare cases killing themselves as they feel there is no way out. It also relates to their sexual activity, should they or shouldn't they. Boys demand blow jobs and the rest, and if girls say no they get called frigid, sluts, slags and are alienated. When they give in to the unrelenting pressure they get called slag, slut, whore and get alienated. And this slut shaming is a game girls join in too.

Our education environment is a misogynistic bear pit that demands emotional resilience, support and confidence to survive. Part of surviving is getting angry and this manifests in different ways, but let me tell you, when it looks for validation externally we see more and more girls sitting outside the Head's office or in 'turnaround' or exclusion rooms and this is not the answer.

All this to contend with in school time. I have not even mentioned the challenges going on at home, in their community, with siblings, boyfriends, part-time jobs and the ever present social media.

The good news is some girls are like the mystics we talked about earlier. They appear to glide through puberty and their school years relatively unscathed, but they are the minority and tend to have lots going for them: elder siblings showing the way, positive relationship with boyfriend, elder brother looking out for them, supportive and present parents staying close to them and openly communicating with them about this stuff.

But we can be there for them too – this scenario is changeable. At Girls Out Loud we see massive shifts in girls' behaviour, mindset, confidence and happiness when we work with them via our intervention programmes and our Big Sister mentoring projects. Role models and professional coaches can help them understand the cause and effect, the external environment and they respond and help them find their voice. It is the most amazing privilege to help change a girl's life and see her confidence grow and her sense of self blossom. Find out how to get involved in the Resources section at the back.

CHAPTER SIX
THE DARK SIDE OF THE INTERNET –
IGNORANCE IS INSANITY

'The internet and technology is
stealing our children's innocence.'

I am a huge fan of the internet and an advocate of social media. It has revolutionised my world and I would be lost without it as would any business in the western world today. I say this while sitting in a remote hillside village in Northern Spain where no one has a mobile phone, kids still play in parks and teenagers meet for coffee and a slice of pizza in the village square, yes they actually communicate face to face! It's like going back in time but idyllic, until I need to communicate with the rest of my world then I am ready to throw my laptop down a ravine in frustration!

Most of us now tweet, text and dabble on Facebook as standard but we are still novices on the functionality of this technology compared to teenagers today who have grown up with the internet as a constant and do not see it as magic like we do, it is just standard and intrinsic to their culture. Also the pace of this technological change is so fast we are struggling to keep up and this means we do not really understand the pressures or the dangers they subject themselves to every minute of the day and night.

The problem is, if we don't know what they are doing in this virtual world and their teachers are as ignorant and time-poor as we are, then who is the class monitor here? Who is making sure no one gets hurt, bullied, victimised or isolated? Who is making sure they are not talking to strangers, engaging in inappropriate behaviour, doing something they may regret? No one, right? Thought so!

By now we all know cyber bullying has led to umpteen suicides in the UK and around the world; we know social media is a paedophile's playground and we know many grooming gangs use Facebook as a recruiting platform. None of this is news, yet we are no closer to protecting our young people from the dangers. Education is inadequate and not getting through to them, they have this mentality that says 'it won't happen to me' and although parental control software is great for the very young whose only access to this world is via the home PC, once they hit 13 and they have their own smart phone then it is game over!

In the past five years I have seen these issues get worse as the gap widens between what we know as adults about the technology and what they don't know as children about the risk.

I have sat with a 15-year-old girl and listened as she told me she was trapped in a relationship with a 42-year-old man she met on the internet and although she wants to finish it she does not know how to.

I have spent hours encouraging a 14-year-old girl to stop engaging with unknown males on an online chat site as a way of getting some attention and easing her loneliness.

I have explained to many groups of girls why it is dangerous to post sexy pictures on your Facebook timeline and I have spent hours using scare tactics about why you should not accept a friend request unless the person really is a friend. Just because his profile says he is 15 and lives in your town does not mean this is true.

It never stops and neither does the internet. It is on 24/7 and very quickly becomes an addiction. It is a way of collecting fake friends, a place for attention and validation, a constant noise in an empty house, anonymous popularity for unpopular kids, and the chance to be someone else if the real you is full of self-hatred and anger.

Most savvy teenagers today very rarely use Facebook as their main communicator – if your mum's on it, it is no longer cool! They communicate through instant messenger apps like Black-berry Messenger and Snapchat, which are impossible to moni-tor unless you have 24-hour access to their mobile phone. And the current trend for anonymous question and answer web-sites like Ask.fm, Spring.me and Qooh is seriously worrying. Here teenagers create a profile, including a picture, and other users can send them anonymous questions without revealing who they are. A recipe for disaster and a playground for un-monitored, extreme sexualised bullying. Here is a mother of a 13-year-old girl talking to the Everyday Sexism project this year:

'I asked my daughter if I could have a look at her profile on Ask. fm and the questions came thick and fast, aggressive, overtly sex-ual and from boys claiming to be from her school. "Have you ever sucked dick?" "Do you shave your pubes?" "What is your bra size?" "Have you done anal?" "Can I bang you?" "Is your c**t dry?" They call her a whore and a slut and make sexual demands like "eat my penis" then threaten her with comments like "I'd like to put a nail gun to your face." And even ask her to upload a video of herself cutting herself!'

It is hard to comprehend that this is going on and that girls are silent about it, but it has become so normal to them and if they do speak up they risk losing their status, their friends, their access to this technology if they get their mobile phone confiscated (which is a threat worse than death!) and they will be singled out in school for all the wrong reasons.

The internet, porn and sexual harassment are interlinked. Girls would not post sexy pictures of themselves online if boys did not demand it or they did not think it was acceptable and what was expected of them as sexy girls. We would not see a new app appear every month to help them look even more sexy if sexy was not the currency by which they are judged. Enter Facetune, the latest app that allows you to Photoshop and edit pictures in an instant before you post them to social media. We would not see sexual violence increases among our young if they were not getting their cues from porn. We would not be in the midst of a silent sexual harassment crisis if girls understood the definitions and boundaries which are sadly lacking in porn material and a lot of the time in mainstream media.

WE ADVOCATE SILENCE WHEN IT COMES TO SEXUAL HARRASSMENT EVEN AT AGE 14!

We teach girls to be silent. We say you must be sexy, sexy is cool, sexy is in – look at the magazines, look at MTV, look at Cheryl Cole and Kim Kardashian, Miley Cyrus and Rhianna. We say your status and value is in your appearance, but with this comes male attention and sometimes it gets a little bit out of hand because you have become too sexy and they cannot control themselves, so they may get violent to teach you a lesson, or they might tell everyone else how naughty you were to put you back in your place. But you asked for it, it is your fault, because you were too sexy; so girls, sometimes you may need to pull it back, cool it down, step back for a bit, give the boys some room. They are only human. If you post pictures of yourself online in your new tight dress, what do you expect? If you get a bit tipsy at the school prom and you end up on the dance floor 'shakin ya booty' like Beyoncé, you are asking for it. This is why so few rape cases result in convictions, as most of the time it's the girl's fault and the boys are never sure whether you like it like this or not anyway, 'cos you do in the movies, so don't bother reporting it, just wait, you will feel better soon.

Some recent entries to the EveryDay Sexism project prove my point:

'14-year-old girl: After splitting up with my first boyfriend, another boy hit on me when I'd been drinking whilst we were out. I said I didn't want to go but he pulled me into the woods and lay me down in a ditch. He started to put his hands down my knickers and I told him no. He pressed his fingers to my lips and whispered me to "shh" like I was a child. I was a child. I think I let him do that because I didn't really know what was right or wrong. I didn't know how to act, I didn't know if I was making a big deal, or being frigid. I never told anyone.'

'Having been raped twice as a teenager, by boys I knew, I always thought I was the problem. Since reading Everyday Sexism I have learnt I was not. I felt guilty for all the events. And girls should be taught things like that rape isn't only stalking a stranger down a dark alley, but taking advantage of a vulnerable girl, and how to recognise and understand when they are doing so.'

'At age 18 after going out with a long-term close friend to a party I stayed over at his. I slept on the floor and crashed out with exhaustion. I woke up with his fingers inside me. I had no idea how to react. So I waited it out.'

Do you see what we are doing? Do you understand what we are saying to girls? I know for many people this is shocking. I have been there and have driven home from many school sessions in tears, barging through the door blubbing to my husband 'How did this happen, how did this happen?'

But believe me when I say we can change this, we can make a difference. Most schools run educational sessions on personal safety, the dangers of grooming and staying safe on social media. Some girls listen, most of them are barely present in the room when this talk is going on because a) they never think it is going to happen to them and b) there are boys in the room and it is uncool to be concerned about this stuff. It is not personal enough, the trainer/teacher is not really talking to them, it is boring!

When Girls Out Loud works with vulnerable girls we are up close and personal, we discuss these issues in small groups when and only when we are in rapport. We have real discussions with the girls about what they are doing, what constitutes a good relationship, how to stay safe but still have fun and we share examples of what can happen if they are not vigilant, and sometimes use scare tactics to get them to see the dangers of their blasé attitude to risk. We can do this and have an impact because the girls feel safe with us, there are no boys in the room to judge them, they have a personal relationship with us and they know we care about them and are not there to judge them. In many cases we offer one-to-one coaching sessions after this session to be there for any girls who need to disclose something or just run something by us and we see a massive difference in the way girls take care of themselves and each other after these sessions. School is a place of learning, it is neither equipped nor set up to deal and cope with the number of social issues arriving through the gate every morning.

I wanted to give the last word on this section to a secondary science teacher and a form tutor in a school in Yorkshire, UK who posted this on the Everyday Sexism site this year:

'I witness on a daily basis the girls in my class being called whore, bitch, slag, slut as a matter of course, heckled if they dare to speak in class, their shirts forcibly undone and their skirts being lifted and held by groups of boys. I want to emphasise that this is more often than not a daily event, and often borders on assault. On a daily basis I am forced to confiscate mobile phones as boys are watching hardcore porn videos in lessons and I have noticed sadly that as time has gone on the girls in my classes have become more and more reserved and reluctant to draw attention to themselves.

'I am currently dealing with a situation whereby a girl in my form class sent a topless photo of herself to her then boyfriend, said boyfriend then used this to blackmail the girl into giving him oral sex which he filmed on his phone and then distributed both the photo and the film to all the boys in his year. This girl is now having to consider leaving the school and interrupting her GCSEs due to the abuse she is experiencing from her fellow pupils.

'What I am seeing every day is incredibly worrying and distressing. It is getting worse and worse. I wanted to share this snapshot of my working life with others. The problem is that other people are too willing to brush this issue under the carpet and dismiss it as just natural teenage deviance. However, being on the front line and dealing with this day after day I can tell you this is a completely different animal. There is an underlying violent and vicious attitude towards girls, a leaning towards seeing them as products to be used.'

My work with girls tends to focus on secondary school age so I have always been comforted in my belief that having survived this part of the journey life would get better once they arrived at university or started work. Think again Jane...

CHAPTER SEVEN
IT GETS BETTER AT UNIVERSITY, RIGHT?

'Campus is a misogynistic bear pit where
only the strong walk away unharmed.'

My personal experience of working with girls at university is limited. I have mentored a few girls in this age bracket and have witnessed my daughter's journey, but nothing could prepare me for what I uncovered. I was and remain horrified – absolutely, completely and utterly horrified.

Maybe I was naïve to think that as the first female students were accepted into Cambridge University in 1873 the battle of the sexes would be over in the halls and debating arenas of higher education. How wrong I was.

The sexual abuse, harassment and exploitation starts during Freshers' Week, their very first week on campus and it never lets up. I draw on the sound work carried out by Laura Bates at the Everyday Sexism project here, who spent months travelling around universities in the UK interviewing young women and encouraging them to speak out about their experiences.

The whole point of Freshers' Week is to introduce new students to the area, each other and university life, and if the events during this week are anything to go by young women have a pretty good idea what they have let themselves in for by the end of the festivities. Here is an example of a few event titles:

Rappers & Slappers

Slag & Drag

CEOs and Corporate Hoes

Golf Pros and Tennis Hoes

As both men and women are expected to dress appropriately for these events it is clear how women are positioned from day one. This is not banter, this is misogyny at its worst. Men are all powerful and women are just seen as meat, sexually available meat. Nice!

The induction to university life continues with some of the most degrading incidents of sexism I have ever come across. Like the boys working behind the Students' Union bar running a competition called 'F**k a Fresher'; there is a point scoring system too if she is a virgin and you could prove it by showing the other guys her knickers. This game is so widely acknowledged throughout the university sector it has different nicknames including Sharking and Seal Clubbing.

What actually happens on these so-called fun night outs is shaming.

'One of the initiations into a social club within the first month of uni was to down a bottle of beer that a man was holding between his crotch. To say no is to be seen as a wet blanket as everyone is on the sidelines cheering on.'

'An event organised by our halls of residence was a "girls and guys" pub crawl. We were split into one group of guys and one of girls and sent off on different pub routes. All the girls were encouraged to wear pink and dress "slutty". We also had to come up with a slut name and write this across our breasts. Upon arriving at each bar one of the older students would shout a word which was code for us to flash either our "tits" or our "arse" or dance in a seductive way in front of the men in the pub. I refused to take part in this and was told I was being too uptight and not getting into the spirit of Freshers' Week. The whole thing culminated in the "girls and guys" meeting up in the Students' Union, where we were informed the older students had organised a competition *with prizes. One prize was for the "slut" who collected the most ties from the guys and one for the "lad" who collected the most bras from the "sluts". I walked out on a scene of drunk male students forcefully taking bras off the female students.'*

And to say the rape culture is alive and well is an understatement. In 2011 Exeter University society printed a 'shag mag' containing an article about how many calories men could burn in the course of stripping a woman naked without her consent. Elsewhere a student was given a set of rules when he joined the university lacrosse team. It included the instruction: 'Members don't date, that's what rape is for'.

During Freshers' Week in 2013 a video was posted online showing 80 student leaders at St Mary's University in Canada chanting:

Y is for your sister

O is for oh so tight

U is for underage

N is for no consent

G is for grab that ass

This was swiftly followed by a poster campaign advertising an event at Cardiff University featuring a T-shirt with the slogan 'I was raping a woman last night and she cried'. Meanwhile a nightclub in Leeds promoted an event called Fresher's Violation with an online video in which a presenter asked a male student 'How are you going to violate a fresher tonight?' He replied 'She's gonna get raped.'

Enough yet? I felt physically sick when I first read this stuff. How can this be in the 21st century after a long battle for our right to education and proof beyond measure we deserve it as we are as bright and as capable as the boys? Is this the problem? And why do the institutions allow this behaviour?

Let's review some key stats:

One in seven female university students has experienced a serious physical or sexual assault during their time as a student. NUS Hidden Marks Survey 2010

Nearly 70% of female university students have experienced verbal and nonverbal harassment in and around their institution. NUS Hidden Marks Survey 2010

Many young people view violence as a normal aspect of an intimate relationship. Wood et al., Standing on my own two feet, London NSPCC 2011

12.7% of girls aged 16-19 have experienced domestic abuse in the last year. British Crime Survey 2010

And sad to say the ill-treatment of young women does not stop with their fellow male students. The examples of sexual harassment and sexist behaviour from eminent professors and teaching staff would make your toes curl. More real stories from the Everyday Sexism project reveals the extent of the toxic environment we are expecting our young women to navigate through in order to enter the professions where we are clearly not wanted nor welcomed:

'On my first day at Cambridge University, an ancient don asked whether I had to "bend over" to get in.'

'Male registrar at college would not have recognised any female students' faces. Our chests? No problem.'

And God be with the brave women who have answered the call to study in traditional male subjects like science, maths, IT and engineering. They come in for some extra special treatment...

'At a freshers' lunch organised by the Physics Society: 'This will be mainly a chance for you to scope out who's in your department and stake your claim early on the one in five girls.'

'I was in a lecture last week on IT systems. The lecturer put up a slide of five talking heads – people like Mark Zuckerberg and the founder of Google and discussed their net worth. He then pointed to the last picture – a blonde, attractive woman. He said: "I put this one up especially for the girls. Anyone know who she is? (silence). Well this is the late Steve Job's wife – now worth x billion by virtue of the man she married. So girls, stick to the IT guys – you never know, you might strike it rich".'

I am silenced by this one. Seriously, how are they getting away with this behaviour? Maybe the next example explains how:

'I went to a talk at my university by an esteemed male professor who was giving advice on how to be a scientist. He said that if we want to succeed in academia as a scientist we needed "male traits" those being competitiveness, confidence and impatience. Also mentioned that having children may be problematic career wise unless we had very understanding husbands. One female academic challenged him afterwards at question time and got dismissed. I left feeling very sad indeed.'

I am with ya gal! Not only would I have felt sad, I would have felt angry, cheated and ready to walk. But this is not the answer is it? And since when has impatience and confidence been the exclusive domain of men? How do we expect our bright young women, the next generation of leaders and law makers and innovators to blossom in this environment? Do they have to develop thick skins and a special kind of immunity to stay the course? Does it become blasé after a while or is their confidence permanently leaking as they come to terms with being viewed as the class sexual object where anything goes? University is supposed to be an enlightening time when we discover ourselves, shape our identities and immerse ourselves in learning subjects we are passionate about before making our way into the world of work. We are being denied the complete experience.

'I had an IT lecturer who would always sit very close on the bench to point out things you did wrong in your program (with casual touches etc). I declined his invitation to an advanced programming group because I knew it was him leading the group. My friend joined it and was constantly groped but she suffered in silence because she wanted to excel at programming.'

And there you have it – succeed and learn but it will cost you your dignity and right to personal space. Can you imagine the uproar if this behaviour took place in our schools or hospitals? Why is it condoned here? It is no surprise that in an environment where casual groping and sexist 'banter' is accepted as normal the risk of serious sexual harassment is high, very high indeed.

'Last year, I was sexually harassed by one of my lecturers. He would routinely invade my personal space, tell me to rub my breast against him, grab me, stare openly at my legs and breasts and talk about sexually explicit topics in class instead of what was on the syllabus. One day after class, he asked me intrusive questions about my sex life to the point where he became visibly aroused. Finally, I told him to back off and he lost his temper with me. I wound up filing a formal complaint after he started throwing away my work instead of returning it to me. I was told by members of staff that sexual harassment is something that happens to women in academia and that I simply needed to learn to put up with it. I was shunned by staff and students alike for being a troublemaker.

'A year on, I'm still dealing with the fallout from the sexual harassment case. I am getting absolutely no support from the university – quite the opposite, in fact. It may sound naïve, but I was shocked that, in 2012, female students at a world-class research university are still treated as second-class citizens and unwanted interlopers in a world created by and for men.'

Me too, me too!

I am delighted to see more and more young women stepping up on campus and creating modern feminist armies to stand up to this, and more importantly to support each other, but what about the people in authority? How do they allow this to continue?

In 2010 a survey of 2,000 female students by the National Union of Students revealed that one in seven respondents had experienced a serious physical or sexual assault during their time as a student. 16% had experienced unwanted kissing, touching or molesting and 68% had been a victim of one or more kinds of sexual harassment on campus. Depressingly only 4% of the students experiencing serious assault reported it to their institution and only 10% reported it to the police. This is due in part to normalising this kind of behaviour and in some cases applauding it! Many young women talk about the fear of even more abuse if they report these incidents and/or the very real unease that they will be blamed and shamed or that somehow it is their fault.

I know you are probably deeply distressed and depressed by this but these stories need to be told and shared. Our young women need protecting and they need to know we are on their side. By the time they get to university they are already indoctrinated into a world that devalues and marginalises everything about them bar their appearance, and what they learn in these great halls of wisdom is more of the same plus a dislike for their brains as well.

I wanted to end this section with the Everyday Sexism entry that made me weep for days for so many reasons. It epitomises the extent of the challenges we face – sexual harassment, rape, abuse of power by men, slut shaming by men and women and fear of police reporting.

'I was 19 and went on a school trip out of town. We all had some drinks and I accidentally locked myself out of my hotel room and knocked on the trip leader's room to get help. I trusted him. He asked me in and, after I had thrown up everywhere, he invited me to sleep in his bed with him. I passed out and woke up to him licking my vagina. I was confused and afraid. In the morning I realised he had raped me while I was unconscious; I was covered in bruises and my vagina and anus hurt. I told the university and several members of staff blamed me for drinking. The rapist told my friends I was a slut and wanted it. No one believed me and people thought I was trying to get attention. That was three years ago and I still haven't reported it to the police.'

CHAPTER EIGHT
WHAT ABOUT THE BOYS, JANE?

'Girls have always moderated boys' behaviour –
not anymore.'

This is a question I get asked on a regular basis: 'What about the boys, Jane, are they lost too?' Whilst I do not dispute this, my passion is focused on the girls for several reasons:

1. I am one, and as such have an affinity to working with and inspiring my own gender. Shoot me!

2. I think boys need male role models and intervention programmes led by men. Refer to point 1.

3. Whilst I accept boys are being fed the same destructive messages through porn and the media about the role and positioning of women, this puts them in control and I think the balance needs shifting.

4. Again, whilst I accept boys can and do suffer from eating disorders, STDs, anxiety and depression, domestic abuse, rape and cyber bullying, the statistics show an overwhelming lean towards girls. Girls have reached crisis point.

5. Boys cannot get pregnant, nor do they feel pressured to accept responsibility for the result of their procreation in terms of financial or parental support.

6. Girls have always moderated boys' behaviour in the playground and the classroom. This has shifted in the past few decades. The natural order worked perfectly with boys showing off their male prowess to impress us girls and us deciding whether it was worthy of our attention and love or not. It was innocent teasing but

both parties understood the rules and enjoyed the chase. Now things have turned nasty as boys have stepped up as rulers not moderators and there is no one moderating their behaviour anymore. Girls need to understand and recognise they hold the key to their own sexual freedom. If we can restore the traditional order by empowering the girls, boys AND girls will be more secure.

7. Success is about what you say no to. I am clear about my niche and will not be swayed or tempted to dilute my brand; however, if anyone knows of a successful organisation doing similar work to us in the UK, working exclusively with boys, I would love to hear from them. We could make sweet music together!

I know there are lots of nice boys out there. I simply could not live in the world if I believed all men and boys were misogynistic pigs and I have enough experience at 50 to know this is not true. And I am pretty sure it must be very uncomfortable for them to stand up against this sexist onslaught too, but they must and we must help them.

RAISING BOYS TO RESPECT GIRLS – A GIVEN RIGHT?

Now as I mentioned before, I am not going to create Boys Out Loud anytime soon but as I am sure you can guess I do have some concerns about the way we are raising our boys.

My main anxiety focuses around this:

Does parenting take account of the major shifts created by feminism? Or are we still raising boys to view girls as home makers, child bearers and sexual objects ONLY? I wonder... As working women do we pass on different values now and teach boys to respect girls, work alongside them and interact with them at all levels? I am not sure...

Are we still empowering boys to be strong, non-emotive, aggressive breadwinners and if so how does this prepare them for an equal relationship with a girl who has the same aspirations as them? Or how would they cope if they were expected to work for a female boss? Or their girlfriend brought home more money than them?

I think we know the answers to these questions, don't we? Society may be changing but very few boys arrive at puberty without some negative or confused presuppositions about the role of women, how to treat them and what they are for. Often they share the same views and believe their world is the same as the one their father or in some cases their grandfather grew up in, whereas girls have very little in common with the world their mothers or grandmothers were raised in. It feels like boys and girls are miles apart in terms of their cultural development and boys definitely need to play catch up.

In a society where the majority of boys will end up in a dual income relationship, co-owning a house, earning similar money and working the same hours as their female mate, how are they going to view this as a partnership when we have brought them up to believe that everything to do with their life outside of work is not their concern? As overprotective superwomen and guilt mothers we have done everything for them since they could walk and talk. They understand very little about keeping house, cooking, shopping, caring for others, managing household budgets etc. We simply expect them to move from the care of mother to wife in one seamless manoeuvre!

From my work in schools it seems to me girls are travelling along the equality and shifting identity highway either alone or with a reticent passenger and this hampers aspiration, it is confusing and will send us all backwards if we do not act now.

Just like girls, boys need more empowering role models. Modern men who believe in and respect the contribution women make to the workplace and the boardroom; men who are already in loving and supportive relationships with women where daily chores are shared or managed as a team and this includes all things domestic, life planning and childcare. I can hear you shouting from here: 'Ha! Yeah right, where are these men then?' Maybe this is part of the problem? Dare I say even men of our generation are struggling with this changing landscape too?

So where does this leave us? It means the shifts need to start with our sons, now, today. We need to go back a generation and teach them to respect girls' brains as opposed to just their 'hot rating'.

This applies to all of us – mothers, sisters, aunties, nannies and friends. Here are my top tips for what I think we need to do now. I am pretty sure you could add to this, please do!

- We must encourage boys to have girls as friends so they are not afraid of encounters with the opposite sex and learn to recognise, acknowledge and respect our differences and our value as early as possible.

- We must not allow them to opt out of all things deemed domestic and women's work. Why are we even thinking of doing this? Keeping house is a joint responsibility; they need the basics like we do.

- We must stop 'overnurturing' them, i.e. doing everything for them as long as they live under our roof. This teaches them nothing (other than it is what women do), it sabotages self-sufficiency and sets them up for a shedload of domestic conflict when they do finally leave the nest to embark on a relationship. We need sisterhood in this!

- We must ensure they have some positive male influences from men that respect women, have some emotional intelligence and get our contribution. These men DO exist, honest, but you may need to look outside your immediate circle to engage them. I have many in my life including my husband, but interestingly enough none in my immediate family, although I see my 16-year-old nephew as a work in progress!

If you have a spare 20 minutes watch Colin Stokes' latest TED talk How Movies Teach Manhood, it is very interesting.

MUM AND DAD – SOON TO BE EXTINCT!

I am also aware and concerned at the number of boys growing up with absent fathers. This is not good news for any of us.

This headline caught my eye last month: **400,000 Women in Britain Do Not Know the Identity of The Father of Their Children.** Even more disturbing was the by-line: **and around 1.2 million fathers insist they are unsure if they really are the dad of their sons or daughters.**

Now I know why Jeremy Kyle has become an institution.

Seriously? Are we living in one gigantic, free-for-all commune? Whatever happened to parenting and responsibility? You may feel I am being a tad judgemental here but I work with vulnerable, troubled teenage girls for a living and let me assure you that lack of or a confused identity is a key player in many of their challenging behaviours, including rebelling, self-doubt, self-harming, rejection, promiscuity, drug use, truancy, looking for external validation via gangs and crime etc. It is important to know who you are and this includes the identity of your father!

Whilst I have no doubt there are some awesome, responsible and inspiring single mums out there and equally awesome fathers raising other men's children, is this the blueprint we want to pass on to the next generation? Children should be conceived in a loving relationship by two consenting adults who accept responsibility for them for life. Anything less sets them up for some uncomfortable conversations and discoveries as they hit puberty and start to ask questions.

Now I know we don't live in a perfect world and mistakes happen and most people do the best they can in some very difficult situations, but surely we must strive to be responsible adults? To say 'Well, I am not sure who your father is, he could be one of three, either an old work colleague, a guy I had a one-night stand with on holiday or John who I was with for three years but left me for another woman' is hardly comforting to a 13-year-old who is starting to question his or her self-worth and identity and looking for answers.

Children of single mums have a tendency to become single mums; children from broken families struggle to sustain long-term relationships or do not know how to create one; and children from complicated home environments with siblings who have different dads or several stepdads and grandparents as guardians can be lost and struggle with authority figures.

We all grow up with the values imprinted on us from our home environment and our parents, breaking them is a tough job and demands some sort of intervention; many young people will not get this kind of opportunity and so the cycle continues on repeating itself.

Being a parent is the most important job in our society; until we recognise this and start to value it, change will be slow or non-existent and we will continue to see our young people enter a full-on identity crisis in their teen years. The strong will survive but what of the vulnerable or the weak?

I am not in the game of alienating men or boys. Not all boys are sexist and not all men are feminists. I am also not an advocate of women ruling the world – how utterly boring! I am a fan, a raving fan of equality. I want our sons and daughters to live together in a world where we work and live in harmony sharing life choices, opportunities, parenting, financial desire and fun. I want us to celebrate our differences, be grounded in our male and female energy and be true. I want us to respect ourselves and each other and work as a team.

This may sound like a fairy tale and if it does I am a princess once more as this defines my relationship with my husband perfectly.

If you are the mother of a son, this one is for you! It is an entry from the Everyday Sexism project from a 17-year-old boy:

'I started following Everyday Sexism and was shocked by what women go through all the time. I started noticing it more and pointing it out. I think some friends listen but the most opposition I've had is at home. My mum tells me to "man-up" when I try to discuss sexism and that there is something "wrong with me" when I pull up my older brother (who is very into all the lad culture) on sexism. She said I'll never get a girlfriend because they want "real men" not ones who "act like girls" and said I shouldn't be bothered about sexism because it doesn't affect me and to stop being "a whining girl". My dad encourages me and my brother to harass women on the street so my brother now does this all the time. I'm not letting it stop me because all the stories I have read are terrible and talking to girls at school they all say they experience sexism regularly but can't believe how much my family and especially my mum hates me caring about it.'

CHAPTER NINE
WHO IS RESPONSIBLE AND
WHERE ARE THE ROLE MODELS?

'Time to step up and show them another way.'

Part of me feels ashamed that we have arrived at this place in the 21st century. A place where girls are not safe, are silenced, invisible and in pain. We encourage them to study so they can enter the misogynistic bear pit that is university, and if they survive that then we entice them further with the promise of a top job in industry, but we do nothing to prepare them for the endemic sexism they will experience or the tough choices they will be forced to make if they expect to get to the top. We fail to mention the downside, we fail to understand or even recognise the impact porn and/or the internet is having on their identity and we allow them to be seduced by reality TV right in front of our eyes. No wonder they are opting out, looking to marry a footballer, choosing safer and less demanding career choices, getting pregnant or queuing up for hours for their three minutes of fame on The X Factor!

We have sent them out to conquer the world ill-equipped to deal with the unacceptable levels of sexism and harassment. In fact, worse than that we are not even facing up to this blatant sexism, we are in denial and hoping if we keep our heads down and prove our worth, over and over and over again, it will somehow disappear. It will not. If we accept the status quo, how are we empowering them? We need to step up, be counted and be the role models they are crying out for. Clearly, we cannot change their environment – well, not effectively or fast enough anyway. The trashy media, the internet, porn, social media, cosmetic surgery and misogyny are all out of the box and we will struggle to put them all back in, in our lifetime. But this is not a good enough reason to do nothing.

Believe me when I say I have gone over and over and over the solutions to this predicament in my head, in my sleep, and in every waking moment since my eyes were opened to this crisis back in 2008 and I can only see one solution:

- We need to educate our girls on the real deal, show them a better way, help them to uncover their natural beauty, their unique gifts and empower them to say no, enough, not now, not ever! And encourage them to support each other as opposed to staying silent or being complicit in their own exploitation.

- We need to inspire them to think big, to believe in their potential and to follow their own path, but we must not mislead them to believe everything in the world of work and higher education is rosy. If we do this we are cheating them and we may as well pull the ladder up behind us now.

- We need to invite real female role models to step up and inspire the next generation with their stories, their successes and their journeys of hope. Train these women to be mentors, advocates and coaches to facilitate and deliver intervention programmes, motivational events and Big Sister mentoring programmes for girls in schools and colleges throughout the UK.

- We need to make sure our girls know we see them, we hear them and what they say matters. Give them the validation they are crying out for, help them to find their voice, self-respect and sisterhood. Help them to shine.

It really is that easy. I know, because along with a team of awesome women and a volunteer posse of thousands, Girls Out Loud has been doing this since 2009 with amazing results.

Remember, children copy adults, if they don't see it, they don't believe it's possible. How are you showing up for them and what are you teaching them about possibility and potential?

THE ENCORE
HOW WAS IT FOR YOU?

My aim at the beginning of this process was to ensure I did not disappear in a puff of smoke when I hit the milestone of 50 – as if! I wanted to share my journey, and more importantly my lessons, so that the things I know for sure could act as a guide or a map for others. It was important to me to speak from the heart, to be honest, to be real, to be me.

Although I have shared my personal story many times in public, committing it to paper was a profoundly emotional process. I had to delve much deeper into my memory banks than ever before and in doing this I was rewarded with insights and nuances I had previously overlooked or refused to see.

Many of my fellow writing friends assured me it would be a cathartic process, but truly it was not. I cried for my mother as I documented her abuse towards me and uncovered her past; I pitied my father as I understood his emotional flaws; and I felt sadness at the loss of my relationship with my sister. I felt truly blessed as I recalled my first meeting with Tony and grieved all over again for the people who are no longer in my life. By the end of the first chapter I was exhausted! I spent many sleepless nights remembering the people who had a huge impact on my life, wondering where they are now and musing over my treatment of them in my story. Was I fair? Did I recall the events with clarity or is my version biased? I concluded it was. I know memories are like beliefs, they are clouded and created by our experience and the emotions we attach to those experiences, so sometimes facts become a little blurry. I just have to hope you will forgive me for this human weakness. It is my story, my version and my reality. I cannot change that.

My roller coaster life, packed with critical moments, was the backdrop for sharing my universal life lessons, my top 10 must haves, all leading to one place: AUTHENTICITY. The end game, the Holy Grail, the purpose of all personal development and growth. The journey to this peaceful place takes a lifetime to master, it demands courage and tenacity as the road is often bumpy, sometimes steep, often veering off into temporary dead ends, only to get back on to racetrack bends and helter-skelter drops! To be authentic means letting go of striving for perfection, giving up worrying about what other people will think, dumping superwoman, saying goodbye and good riddance to the eternal people pleaser in us and embracing our vulnerability, shame and flaws. It means saying no when you are expected to say yes and vice versa and it necessitates tuning into your higher self every moment of every day. If you do the work on you by following the other nine principles it gets easier to understand and it becomes the only place you want to live, but be warned, there are no quick fixes to believing you are enough!

When I reflect on my journey I get a sense that I have been slowly but surely guided. Everything that has happened to me for better or for worse has gently nudged me towards my legacy. My critical moments, particularly my failures, have motivated me to excel; my relationships have taught me to trust my intuition; love has taught me forgiveness and patience; and my career path has taught me the value of hard work, independence and the benefits of going the extra mile.

I have collected skills, lessons and learnings like a magpie, which in turn has given me resilience, credibility, a track record, calmness in the shadow of failure and a personal brand.

I would never have become a coach without serious investment in my own personal development and being able to get closure on my own story, nor would I have developed a Divapreneur Mindset programme without having spent many years becoming one. And how is it possible to connect at an emotional level with women and girls from all walks of life without a passion for female empowerment and human potential, an empathy for the road less travelled, and an instinct for doing the right thing, not necessarily the easy one or the one in view?

And for the record, how would I recognise superwoman if I had never worn the cape? Today, in the words of Brene Brown I consider myself a recovering perfectionist and an aspiring good enoughist!

My journey to authenticity continues as I continue to do the work. My peer group expands at the same pace as my horizons; I have several mentors in my life at any one time; I read and invest in seminars and conferences and it remains impossible to stand still when your job is about inspiring others to step up and shine. Kinda keeps ya on ya toes!

This book is also about my passion to encourage women the world over not to forsake feminism. We need it today more than ever, the playing field is nowhere near level and as our society becomes more and more misogynistic I can assure you our sisters of old would be chaining themselves back to those railings if they could see what we are putting up with in the playground, on campus, in the workplace, in the media and in our public places.

Now is not the time to take our foot off the gas, now is the time for frame-breaking change, we need legislation and we need to stop putting our faith in a meritocracy that does not exist unless you are male, part of the young or old boys' network or happy to go native.

We need to believe in ourselves and know for sure we can create and lead big businesses, take a seat on the board and attract men that are worthy of us and we need to recognise the power in unity and put sisterhood back on the agenda.

This will not happen until we recognise the unrelenting and unreasonable pressure we have put on ourselves to be perfect in every way as a direct result of buying into media messages that tell us we need to subscribe to a cloned version of beauty and spend thousands of pounds and hours to stay looking young and skinny.

When you consider the teen girl crisis we are in the midst of we have to ask ourselves how are we showing up for them? Or are we part of the problem? If we accept workplace sexism as banter and fail to report sexual harassment for fear of being seen as 'arsy', or if we pop along for Botox in our lunch hour and pop pills to lose that stubborn stone to get bikini fit, are we any better than the Z list celebrities they aspire to?

This is a bright young woman ranting, rightly so, about media objectification, cultural dismissal and prevalent abuse in her world, our world, the 21st century:

'I'm sick of walking home from university at 6pm and getting harassed every time; from people shouting things or making fellatio gestures out of their cars because they think they're funny or that I should be "flattered", or the people in the street who make kissing noises when I walk past, or shout "slut"' or "get ya tits out" at me. Flattering? How is that flattering? I'm on the verge of tears every time I get home.

'When I go to a club, no matter if I wear something modest, or something that society deems "sluttish" I will get grabbed by someone who thinks by doing so I'll find them attractive, or I should take it as a compliment. I'm left feeling violated and as if it's my fault. Because I'm a woman? Because I'm in a dress? Because I should be expecting it?

'I'm tired of my voice being undermined because of my gender. I'm tired of having a man explain to me that I'm overreacting, when he has no idea what it's like. I'm tired of being told when I'm angry that I'm a pushy bitch, or that I must be menstruating. I'm tired of being called a slut, because I have sex, or because I don't have sex and reject the advances of some man in a club. I'm

tired of having to watch my behaviour, watch what I wear, what I drink, where I go and be extra careful to avoid harassment or worse, which is just going to happen no matter what do. I'm tired of watching women be blamed for rape, that they should have seen it coming, shouldn't have drunk so much, shouldn't have worn that, could have prevented it, didn't shout loud enough, didn't fight back hard enough.

'How can I believe the people that say women have equal rights? When the worst insult a man can be called is a woman, girly, a twat, a tit, a c**t, that he needs to "man-up" and the list goes on. My gender is not an insult. I am tired of all this s**t.'

Are you?

When we acknowledge there is a problem and make the changes, then we will become the role models our teen girls need and the talent pipeline will be invigorated with smart, sassy, 'take no s**t' young women destined for the top, in control of their careers with equality as their mantra in and out of work. Arrgh! Joy!

We need to be kinder to ourselves and each other and reserve our anger for those people who are hurting us and our daughters. We need to know for certain we are already enough and we deserve our success. Time to stop beating ourselves up and start a new chapter. One where the authentic you is welcome and is allowed to shine.

I hope my musings, my rants, my lessons and my insights have given you food for thought and maybe opened your eyes to a crisis that demands sisterhood to banish. My intention was never to hurt or offend, I set out with a passion to help women recognise what they need to do to shine and create a better world for our daughters, and I hope I have stayed true to my goal.

Until we meet again on twitter or face to face I wish you well and hope you will support the Girls Out Loud cause, we all have a responsibility to pass on our learnings to each other and the next generation.

So, invest in you, find your voice, rock your world and pass it on!

To end here is a quote I stole and tweaked from one of my spiritual gurus Louise Hay. It has become the Diva mantra and I give it to you with love.

Inside of you
Is a smart and powerful
Dynamic and capable
Self-confident, alive and alert
Fabulous Diva!
Let her come out to play
The world is waiting for you

RESOURCES & REFERENCES

I am a fanatical reader but this is not an academic journal so I have avoided the detailed bibliography and referencing thing! Here are some of the books and resources that have informed my writing and may be worth a second glance.

BOOKS

About Business:

The E-Myth Revisited. Why Most Small Businesses Don't Work and What to do About it by Michael E Gerber. Published by Harper Business Books 2001

The Icarus Deception by Seth Godin. Published by Penguin Group 2012

The Dip by Seth Godin. Published by Penguin Group 2007

Tribes by Seth Godin. Published by Penguin Group 2008

In fact anything by Seth Godin. The man is a visionary and a genius!

Your Life, Your Legacy by Roger Hamilton. Published by Achievers International 2006

The Long Tail by Chris Anderson. Published by Random House Business Books 2006

Key Person of Influence by Daniel Priestley. Published by Ecademy Press 2010 (now Panoma Press)

Business Stripped Bare by Richard Branson. Published by Virgin Books 2008

About Women:

The Equality Illusion by Kat Banyard. Published by Faber & Faber Limited 2010

How To Be A Woman by Caitlin Moran. Published by Ebury Publishing 2011

Why Women Mean Business by Avivah Wittenberg-Cox & Alison Maitland. Published by John Wiley & Sons Ltd 2008

See Jane Lead: 99 Ways For Women To Take Charge At Work by Lois P Frankel PhD. Published by Warner Business Books 2007

Fifty Shades of Feminism. Edited by Lisa Appignanesi, Rachel Holms & Susie Orbach. Published by Virago Press 2013

Lean In - Women, Work and the Will to Lead by Sheryl Sandberg. Published by Ebury Publishing 2013

The Gifts Of Imperfection by Brene Brown. Published by Hazelden 2010

Beyond The Boys Club by Suzanne Doyle-Morris PhD. Published by Wit and Wisdom Press 2009

The Miseducation of Women by James Tooley. Published by Continuum Books 2002

Not That Kind of Girl by Lena Dunham. Published by Forth Estate 2014

Unspeakable Things - Sex, Lies and Revolution by Laurie Penny. Published by Bloomsbury Publishing USA 2014

About personal development:
Heal Your Life by Louise L Hay. Published by Hay House Ltd 2002

A Return To Love by Marianne Williamson. Published by Harper Collins Publishers 1992

Power of Intention by Dr Wayne W Dyer. Published by Hay House 2004

Think & Grow Rich by Napoleon Hill. Published by Wilshire Book Company 1999

7 Strategies for Wealth & Happiness by Jim Rohn. Published by Prima Publishing 1985

About girls and young women:
Living Dolls The Return of Sexism by Natasha Walter. Published by Virago Press 2010

Everyday Sexism by Laura Bates. Published by Simon & Schuster UK Ltd 2014

The Vagenda - Zero Tolerance Guide To The Media by Holly Baxter & Rhiannon Lucy Cosslett. Published by Square Peg 2014

Raising Girls by Gisela Preuschoff. Published by Harper Thorsons 2004

Stripped – The Bare Reality of Lap Dancing by Jennifer Hayashi Danns & Sandrine Leveque. Published by Clairview Books 2011

Female Chauvinist Pigs. Women And The Rise Of The Raunch Culture by Ariel Levy. Published by Simon & Schuster UK Ltd 2005

Overloaded - Popular Culture and Future of Feminism by Imelda Whelehan. Published by Women's Press Ltd 2000

ONLINE STUFF
A few people and organisations worth following:

On twitter
@NoMorePage3

@everydaysexism

@vagendamagazine

@caitlinmoran

@Oprah

@sethgodinblog

@the3rdimagazine – global women in business magazine

@TEDxWomen – a global community of smart women

@Gdnwomensleaders – Guardian community to get more women to the top

@marwilliamson – author, spiritual teacher

@Shequotes – kick ass quotes by amazing women

@Epic_women – celebrating some of the most amazing women ever to walk the planet

A WORD ABOUT STATISTICS

The amount of data available on the issues discussed in this book is endless. I have selected facts to give a good overview and a snapshot to support the content and my passion. I have made every effort to only include facts from reliable sources; however, I am aware I have not exhausted every available statistic so forgive me for any obvious omissions.

ABOUT THE AUTHOR

Jane is 50 and excited to be starting the next act of what has been, so far, an amazing life. She is a serial entrepreneur, intuitive coach, inspirational speaker, youth advocate, keen blogger and writer, ambassador for female empowerment and all round sassy Diva!

For the past 10 years she has worked exclusively with women and teenage girls via two aspirational brands she created: www.wellheeleddivas.com and the social enterprise www.girlsoutloud.org.uk Her passion for potential is contagious and despite many critical moments her courage to live life at the edge of her comfort zone is an inspiration.

You can engage with her today via the following channels:

On twitter @divadomrocks

On Facebook https://www.facebook.com/jane.kenyon.50

On LinkedIn http://uk.linkedin.com/pub/jane-kenyon

On Google+ https://www.google.com/+JaneKenyon1

Follow her blog at http://janekenyon.wordpress.com/

Jane's first book *Superwoman – Her Sell By Date Has Expired. Time to Show Little Miss Perfect The Door* is available to buy at www.wellheeleddivas.com or at Amazon.com.

STEP UP AND BECOME A ROLE MODEL
TODAY WITH GIRLS OUT LOUD

I genuinely hope that this book has motivated you to step up and become a role model for the next generation. In fact, I already know that in buying and reading this book you have an interest in all things female and feel some responsibility to do your bit to ensure equality of opportunity is a given for the next generation. I hope I have demonstrated that we are not there yet and our teenage girls need us now more than ever, to help them find their voice, be bold and shine.

Girls Out Loud is a social enterprise and charity foundation on a mission to do just that by creating and delivering a range of early intervention programmes from two hours to 12 months in duration, in schools throughout the UK. Our work focuses on embedding a more empowering mindset in our girls, increasing confidence, self-esteem and emotional resilience and dealing with the ever present negative body hang-ups and mental health challenges.

The core premise of our work is to introduce the girls to real, sassy, successful female role models who are rocking their world and committed to paying it forward.

Our fastest growing programme is Big Sister, a 12-month mentoring programme where we train women from all walks of life to be a mentor to a girl aged between 13 and 16 for a year.

To find out more about our work, step up and fundraise for us, become a Big Sister, volunteer at our school events or simply help us spread the word, visit www.girlsoutloud.org.uk today or follow us on twitter @girlsoutloudorg

Reviews for SUPERWOMAN

I love this book. I love its honesty, and the fact that Jane delivers the messages - which are sometimes controversial - in her own inimitable, authentic style. Amongst a plethora of material about gender diversity, quotas and boardroom statistics etc, this is the first time I have witnessed someone putting their head above the parapet and admitting that women are not the same as men, we have different needs, skills and strengths and do you know what, it's bloody amazing to be a woman!
Nina Lockwood, Intuitive Recruitment

I read this book in one sitting and found it comforting that I am not the only one struggling with some of the issues and enlightening that I too fall into the superwomen trap on occasion and most importantly some ideas about what to do about it!
Jane Barrett, The Career Farm

I loved Jane's down to earth and engaging writing style and I found I could identify completely with what she was saying. It made me look at my experiences in a different light. In particular, I realised that an unhappy corporate experience was rooted in a clash of male v female energies... if only I'd had the book then, I'd have felt more in control of the situation...
Karen Pheasant, Entrepreneur

This book sheds light on the sad state of affairs that most of us women have bought into and how we are creating impossible role models and worlds for our children to grow up in. It's an easy read that gets under your skin and makes you want to make changes for the better! - A must read book for women in all walks of life!
Cara Leach, Sales Champion

A wonderful book which brings together some useful insights into how us women work. Written with a touch of humour as well as some sound advice for all superwomen out there!
Caroline Wilson Corporate Executive

**Controlling Everything Doesn't Give You Power.
It Gives You A Blinding Headache.
Time To Let Superwoman Go...**

Superwoman is alive and well and strutting around in her stilettos, sabotaging your right to an imperfect life. She is feeding your insecurities, she is damaging your self belief, she is sabotaging your businesses, your careers and your relationships and she is NOT a great life model to pass on to our daughters.

She is what happens when we buy into the modern myth of 'having it all' and she has to go! She empowers us to stay small; shop for things we don't need; obsess over eternal youth and multi task within an inch of emotional exhaustion on a daily basis.

There is a better place to live. One where your authentic soul is nurtured, your vunerability is nourished and you are allowed to be you. Controlling everything does not give you power, it gives you a blinding headache! We need to learn to let go, say no, accept help, stop controlling everything, recognise the power of vulnerability and stop beating ourselves up for failing to hit perfect 24/7.

This book uncovers how superwoman is showing up in your professional life, your business, your marriage, in your role as a mother, in your attraction strategy and in your identity. It is a call out to out to women everywhere to be kinder to each other and ourselves as we step up to reclaim our feminine souls.

Available to buy at www.wellheeleddivas.com

Printed in Great Britain
by Amazon